# Ukraine Adoption
How we did it – How you can too

By Michael Redman

Cover Illustration
Grace Redman & India Redman

Cover Design
India Redman

Edited by Milka Peric, Linda Parker
and India Redman

Copyright 2010
ISBN 978-0-9828378-9-4

# Ukraine Adoption
## How we did it – How you can too

### By Michael Redman

This book is dedicated to my wife Paula, who dreamed of our journey many years ago. Without her energy and compassion for all children, this book would never have been written.

I also want to thank Frontier Horizons for the work they do finding homes for orphaned children; to my new friend Valery (the Melitopol orphanage director) who takes care of the children; to Vitaly, who I believe, would have quite literally given his life to help us adopt our girls; to my daughters, who give me more love than I deserve; to June, whose support allowed us to leave Grace with the assurance that she was truly in good hands; and to Jesus Christ, our inspiration and guide.

# CONTENTS

| | |
|---|---:|
| *Foreword* | 9 |
| *Acknowledgments* | 13 |
| *Children of the World — Grace* | 16 |
| *Ukraine — An Option* | 20 |
| *The Invitation* | 30 |
| *The Journey Begins* | 33 |
| *The SDA Meeting* | 42 |
| *Donetsk, Ukraine* | 48 |
| *SDA Second Meeting* | 58 |
| *Melitopol, Ukraine* | 63 |
| *Nadya and Albina* | 95 |
| *Disbelief* | 109 |
| *Frontier to the Rescue* | 116 |
| *The Eight-Day Dossier* | 122 |
| *Third Trip to Ukraine* | 127 |
| *The Siblings* | 136 |
| *Home for the Holidays* | 161 |
| *The Final Trip* | 180 |
| *Court* | 188 |
| *Orphanage Party* | 203 |
| *Goodbye Ukraine* | 215 |
| *The U.S. Embassy* | 221 |

| | |
|---|---|
| *Home at Last* | *229* |
| *One Year Later* | *231* |
| *Grace's Thoughts About Our Adoption* | *236* |
| *Albina's Story* | *238* |
| *Best Advice and Lessons Learned* | *247* |

# Foreword

I have never before attempted to write a book, or even an article for that matter, and I believe this book, *Ukraine Adoption*, is somewhere in between.

We will never truly understand the Ukrainian people and their struggle. Children are often raised with no supervision and left to fend for themselves. This is a country where casual whistling can draw looks of anger, and the general population lives an average of 15 years or less than their American counterparts. Most Americans will never experience this country where kindness and hardship co-exist.

In Ukraine, we often felt as if we were truly on another planet. Our adoption was an educational, expensive and emotional experience of epic proportions.

This book contains many of the lessons learned from our multiple trips, successes, failures and emotional awakenings — some that were unbelievable. If a book like *Ukraine Adoption* existed, we might have been a little less naive and approached this adventure with our eyes wide open, saving time, money and tears along the way.

Like most people, I didn't know much about Ukraine; a country seemingly stuck in the 1950s where technology takes a back seat to survival and where the people somehow accept their hardships as normal. Their fascination with movie stars, Coca Cola and western fashion, strangely offset manly crew cuts and the generally tough living conditions in all but the largest of cities.

One day, I was talking to a couple of people we'd met who worked in the Ukrainian adoption system and I told them that we had seen firsthand the challenge of keeping correct and current information on all of the orphans. I even offered to develop a national web-based tracking system for *free* in order to share this information among the orphanages — since I'm an IT professional and run a web development company. I expected them to be excited, as their jobs would become easier and more efficient, but what I experienced were simply blank stares, which I interpreted as, "So what, we like this mess just the way it is."

What they actually said was, "The government, the State Department for Adoption and Children's Rights Protections (SDA) and adoption system doesn't have a budget for the Internet." Unfortunately, this is what I term the *non-future* of Ukraine. If they don't get on the technology bandwagon soon, they will never be able to catch up with the rest of the world.

From what we could tell, most of their buildings have not been painted since Ukraine was privatized, and corruption is rampant, which bolsters a suffering economy.

Ukraine has much to offer the world as a supplier of produce, minerals and beautiful women. They just need to step up to the plate, be seen and join the rest of the world economy. There are thousands of children orphaned in Ukraine by some natural cause or left by a parent who drinks too much and cannot feed or take care of them. These children, like many in other countries, need our help — they want and need to be seen.

*Ukraine Adoption* is our story. You may find it interesting — I sincerely hope you do — but most of all, I hope it will be enlightening. I have tried to journal, with some detail, the daily events and their relevance to our adoption saga. It was a long, emotional journey for Paula and I, but my hope is that after reading this book, you may be encouraged to step up to the plate and adopt one of Ukraine's magnificent orphaned children.

The adoption process took four trips to Ukraine over a ten-month period. It also cost us much more than we expected — somewhere in the range of $70,000. We are very fortunate that we could afford the expense, and that my job would allow me to be out of the country for extended periods of time. Your experience will no doubt be very different from ours, but the problems and complexity will most likely be the same.

You should not need to spend $70,000 (or even close to this amount) to adopt in Ukraine. It is actually very affordable, especially if you go through an organization like Frontier Horizons that can help you find a facilitator in Ukraine. If you research carefully, you will save money, time, and reduce the stress that comes with this precious gift you are giving a child… your love, a family, and a future.

*I would ask that you do not copy and send this book to your friends. All of the proceeds from this book will go to our host orphanage in Melitopol and to help care for their children.*

# Acknowledgments

Our story would not be complete without dedicating a few words to the Director of the Melitopol orphanage, Valery, and our local facilitator, Vitaly.

Along the way, I was touched very deeply by these two men. Both of them have big places in their hearts for the lost children of Ukraine.

The first time Paula and I met Vitaly was when we arrived to meet Emma in Donetsk . He had a kind, reassuring smile and spoke very good English. Over the next six months, we watched Vitaly work endless hours, traveling regularly, day after day, trying his best to make us comfortable and guiding us through probably the most complex government process in all of Ukraine — adopting a child.

Like most people in Ukraine, he works extremely hard just to make enough money to feed his family. What we did not know when we first met him, was that he was working in this stressful situation with serious health problems, getting paid a fraction of the typical fee we paid our first facilitator. Vitaly is 48, has had heart surgery, and currently has a heart rhythm issue. Despite these problems, he never complained, even when he should have, and I just could not help wondering why.

There were a couple of reasons Vitaly traveled all night on the train just to get one document signed, work with us all the next day, and then do it all over again. The first is, obviously, that his family needed the money. The other is his huge heart which was broken many years ago when he lost his first child at age seven, due to the poor Ukrainian healthcare system and their indifference.

Vitaly wanted Paula and I to have a child, and for the children to have a family and a home. I know it sounds simple, but he is one smart, focused guy and we will never be able to repay him. Our adoption was extremely complex and most facilitators would have given up. Not Vitaly. He stuck with us the whole time — even helping us when we returned home with no thought of compensation other than helping our girls and us.

The other person that touched me deeply was Valery [the orphanage director]. Somehow, even though we could not communicate without a translator, we became good friends and developed what I hope will be a lasting relationship.

It takes a special kind of person to do what Valery does. He is 68 years old and formally retired eight years ago, although still working seven days a week at the orphanage, and always sporting his suit and tie drawn tightly around his neck.

What I noticed in the first few minutes I spent with Valery was his intense regard for his children. I say *his* children because he is the father figure and caregiver to all of those who end up in his care. When he speaks in that authoritative booming voice, the children all stop and listen — but it is always meant kindly

— whether he says something like, "Paula and Michael are now the parents of Albina and Nadya. They are good people and I know that our girls will be well, ok."

Or doling out punishment, orders, rules, or anything else required by his position .

Valery protected the children even while balancing our friendship and his desire to assist us. He allowed us to break most of the rules — letting us take our girls to town for dinner or to shop, as long as we were back by 7 p.m.

At 7 p.m. sharp, our phone would ring and it would be Valery asking, "Exactly where are my girls and when will you be here?" He would be waiting at the orphanage door like a concerned parent.

All of the teachers and employees listen to Valery as he barks orders or laughs with them — and he always honors them. He understands that he has a responsibility to run this orphanage in the best possible way — and he does so — on pennies. He lives a modest lifestyle. I admire him greatly.

# Children of the World ~ Grace

My wife, Paula, and I decided to adopt our first child in 1999. We wanted to build our own family while saving a child and giving them a future. I won't go into the process of adopting from China, as this book is devoted to our Ukrainian experience, but I can tell you that it was also long and frustrating. The process in China was much more straightforward than Ukraine, but the upfront work and wait was significantly greater. In short, after 19 months, we finally adopted Grace Lila Redman. She was 10-months-old, and couldn't even sit up. Grace is a beautiful, bright, well-adjusted "American girl", as she calls herself, and truly the light of our lives.

When Grace was only 4 years old she regularly asked us "Where is my sister? I want a sister." Paula would smile and say, "We are very happy with you Grace, and you get all of our attention," but this didn't go over very well with Grace and after lots of talking and searching of our hearts, we came to the conclusion that adding another child into the mix might round out our family and help Grace at the same time — not to mention that the world has many children who deserve a chance and a future.

Our first attempt at fulfilling this new mission was in 2005 when Paula found a small agency that worked in Russia. Their promise was that we could have a child in as little as four months after our papers were submitted. Paula worked diligently on our paperwork and had it ready to go in about eight weeks. No record, but still very fast in the adoption world.

In January of 2005, we submitted our papers along with a hefty fee of about $12,000 and waited. We were used to waiting and this was no different than when we adopted Grace, except that we were mentally prepared to go to Russia for six weeks in May. We went about our daily lives, I worked and Paula studied alternative medicine and nutrition, which is her passion. May came before we knew it and we were ready to go… then May went… and so did June, July, August and November. In December, our caseworker contacted us and told us that she finally had a child.

"Unfortunately she is not the age you want. "

"The child was only 10 months old and has a brother." As much as we wanted to make the adoption work the child was too young. Paula and I are well aware of our place in life, what we can handle, our limitations and so forth.

We wanted a four-year-old daughter. One of the reasons was so that Grace would have a playmate, they could go to the same school, and when we were no longer as active in their lives, they would have each other. The child that was offered to us after this extended wait period was an infant with a brother, and she had health issues.

We talked endlessly trying to decide if we could handle this new scenario but in the end, turned down the referral. One thing we have learned through our adoption experiences is that you most certainly will not get exactly what you want or expect with regards to referrals. You will go through the same process we did deciding what will work for you and your family and then, ultimately, you'll make the right decision as we did… on more than one occasion. Hold out for what works for you, and indeed it will.

If you have ever been part of the adoption process, you will understand how attached we were to even the thought of a new child in our lives. We had been preparing for months for this new Russian orphan to join our family, and Paula was crushed. She had worked so hard, from every imaginable angle and God's plan or not, it hurt… for a long time.

~ *One Year Later*

Paula and I somehow knew that we were supposed adopt again, so in early 2007, we decided that we would try one more time and go back to China to find Grace a sister. At least we knew what to expect in China and the agency, "Children of the World," which is run by a wonderful woman named Pat Lee, is straightforward and she truly cares about "her kids" as she calls them, which is much more than I can say about the agency we worked with in Russia.

We approached Pat and told her that we would like to adopt a two- to five-year-old (opening up our options) and she said that that should not be a problem given our age. Paula cranked up the now too familiar paperwork machine and after a short time, we submitted a new dossier to China, again with a new fee. Pat assured us that the wait period would be much shorter than when we had adopted Grace, and she was right.

Six months later we received our referral. In China, you submit your paperwork and the director of state adoption picks a child for you. We had met this man on the last night of our trip to adopt Grace. We had a great dinner together with all seven of the adoptive families and he was our guest. At the time, he was probably 45-years-old and personally matched every child with every couple. That's about 6,000 children per year… a very busy man.

But this time around there was a problem. The child that the director had picked for us was only nine-months-old. We thought that this had to be impossible. Surely at our age, they would not let us adopt an infant *and* we had specifically requested an older child. "Unbelievable," Paula said, as we both fell into a depressed state thinking that adoption was not in God's plan for us. We called Pat right away. "Pat, they sent us an infant. What can we do?" She replied, "This is your child unless you would like to refuse the referral and try again, but you will go back into line." So here we were again.

Paula and I deliberated the pros and cons of adopting an infant. Could we start again from ground zero? Would Grace even relate to her? On and on it went until we came to the conclusion that an infant just would not work for our family. We had lost all confidence in the Chinese system because they obviously didn't even read our petition. As depressing as it was we could not go on — we pulled the file.

# Ukraine [An Option]

In June of 2007, Paula came to me and asked, "What would you think of adopting a little girl from Ukraine? I hear it is very quick and you get to look at a picture and choose your child."

My first reaction, as it sometimes is, was not completely supportive.

"I don't know, honey, we have been at this for years now and I am not sure that we can handle another failed attempt."

"What do you mean OUR AGE? ", she whipped back.

"Well, I don't know about you but I just may not have the energy to go through this again."

"Give it a day and let's talk about it tomorrow," Paula said. She knows me pretty well and that I'd probably come around to her way of thinking — I usually do. I have always been easy-going about most things not related to my work.

The next day, hoping I would give in, Paula said, "I've found an agency that will help us adopt in Ukraine." I could see that I didn't have a chance. "I started the paperwork and think we can get it done pretty quickly because we have so much of the boilerplate paperwork already completed."

I just smiled and said, "Okay, sounds like a plan," knowing that this was how it would turn out anyway and there was no use in even trying my usual tactic of reasoning with her.

Paula had made up her mind to adopt a second child several years ago. When our last attempts in Russia and China failed I thought the pursuit was over. What *I* failed to realize is that it never was really over, just on hold.

For the next couple of months, I worked away at my job, as a software consultant for needy companies, and Paula worked on the paperwork. In September 2007 we completed and submitted our dossier to Ukraine through an adoption agency in Austin, Texas called International Family Services (IFS). They led us on a wild goose chase of paperwork, unnecessary travel, promises and simply were not honest with us.

Even though our dossier had been submitted, there was always just one more paper or more money required to secure our position in the long adoption line. Paula was frazzled from all of the needless "fire drills" she was being put through by the adoption agency each time they would tell us, "We need this or that paper *immediately* in Ukraine" which would require a four-hour drive to Columbus, Ohio to have a paper apostilled and sent FedEx to Ukraine for $221. Frequently, the papers never needed to be prepared in the first place. It seemed like they wanted to keep us engaged and busy so we wouldn't notice how far off we were from their original promise of a child by the end of the year.

We were then told by IFS that we would get our invitation letter very soon to travel to Ukraine in February 2008, so our excitement and anticipation was building once again. We were actually going to go this time. I almost couldn't believe it. In fact, I didn't believe it and was soon proven correct.

February came and went and IFS told us they didn't know when we might go. Our distress was not new to us, as you probably can imagine. Adoption is a noble cause that is not without its own special set of pressures.

*March 2008*
*Cleveland, Ohio*

Paula received an email from our caseworker in early March with a picture of a little girl named Karina attached. When Paula showed me the picture, her face lit up like a Christmas tree.

"This is the girl in my dreams! She is our daughter. Look," as she pointed to a picture she had cut out from a magazine of an Asian and European girl standing next to each other. She was right. Little Karina looked just like the child in the picture.

Paula picked up the phone and called our caseworker.

"We'll take her! I cannot believe you found my daughter!" The caseworker's reply was not at all what Paula expected.

"Well, she's not even in the system yet. She is not available to you for adoption."

Paula was dumbfounded. "What is going on here? Why would they even send us this picture?" The caseworker said it was to show us the kind of child that we could have. We understood later it was probably because they had not delivered on their promise and it was a delay tactic of some kind.

Paula is an amazingly strong woman — even though she will tell you that she is not. She rarely takes "No" for an answer and when she has made up her mind to do something — be warned — do not try to change it.

And so the journey began…

The phone calls over the next few days were fast and furious. "Why can't we adopt her?" Paula said, and the caseworker replied, "Because she is not in the Ukraine adoption system."

"How do we find out when she is adoptable?"

"I'll talk to Konstantin, the facilitator in Ukraine, who can find out." And so it went on for several days. Phone calls and emails back and forth — back and forth

Then, out of nowhere, we started to see blogs and emails about a new law in Ukraine that would directly affect us.

*"There has been a change in the law - There can be no more than 45 years between the adoptive parent and the child."*

Evidently they change the adoption laws annually in the first week of December.

Our new plan was disappearing before our eyes. If this were true, it meant that we could not adopt a child under 11 years old. Ouch, this didn't fit our plan at all, even though it had been changing from the day we started to even envision adopting a second child. Still, Paula would not give up. She kept the emails going to the IFS caseworker.

"The only way we see you doing something here is to take a mission trip to meet the little girl Karina," Konstantin wrote in an email. "If you do this, we might be able to petition for her," (showing total disregard for the new adoption laws).

Not knowing any better, we took the bait. Paula went into overdrive as she started working the plan out in her head.

"Okay, I have it all figured out. I am going to Ukraine to meet this little girl, Karina. I'll take Aunt June, Grace, and our nanny, Helene." We made the reservations the very next day using Paula's frequent flyer miles for June to come to Cleveland from Florida, and for everyone (except me) to travel to Ukraine.

Three weeks later, I said goodbye to my wife at the airport as they all headed on a 10-day mission trip to a small orphanage outside of Odessa in southern Ukraine. The idea was to help the orphanage director in any way she needed, meet Karina, and see if there might be a deal to be made in the process.

As with most things in life, we are not in control of events or outcomes. June, who was 77 at the time, did not have a good trip and was sick when they arrived in Kiev. Both Paula and I were very anxious for her welfare and we worried that the trip might end before it even started.

The girls' driver, Yuro, met them at the airport. He was a tall lanky, young man who was a sailor when he was not driving, as well as a chain smoker with an infectious sense of humor.

After meeting their contact, Konstantin [facilitator], in downtown Kiev, they were off on the seven-hour drive to the orphanage in his clunky old car driving along pothole-ridden roads and getting a visual education along the way. You see, Ukraine has continually deteriorated since its liberation from the former Soviet Union, and the country no longer has the money to take care of its roads, buildings, or anything else for that matter. Poverty is rampant. As a visitor, you see, first-hand, a country trying to recover from decades of neglect.

---

Paula's mission trip in her own words:

"I remember seeing my friend, Martin, when I had a dream about this little girl. She looked a lot like Grace. She had dark hair some Asian features, and she was very small. Then I was talking to our agency IFS and I asked them if they had any children that might have Asian features and she said that there are many children that other people would consider Asian. 'I'll send you some pictures.'

I brought grandma June, Grace and our friend Helene to Ukraine and we used my frequent flyer points to buy the tickets.

On the way to the orphanage in Mykolayiv we saw a little kiosk type store that sold pastries, and the sign above the store said 'Karina'. That was the little girl's name and just another sign for me that this was meant to be.

Then we pulled the car up to the orphanage and I heard these little footsteps run up to the car, By the time I turned around she had disappeared but I knew it was Karina.

The orphanage director was expecting us and stood at the front entrance. It was customary to bring little gifts like ice cream or cookies and additional gifts for the director each time we visited.

The director was a nice woman and willing to let us meet the kids but they would never single out Karina. They would bring her whole class in and Karina came over to me because she knew we were interested in adopting. It was probably 100 degrees outside and she was covered in wool tights so I helped her tuck in her shirt and pull up her skirt. The whole time standing very still with her arms hanging straight down tight at her side. She was so nervous and so hot.

The next day, we visited again and they let us spend a little more time with her. The following day they let us take her off campus down by the Baltic Sea. I remember that she and Grace looked like little butterflies running on the rocks. Karina was just very cute, and vivacious. She would come right back when you asked her questions and nothing fazed her.

**Karina, Paula and Grace**

We had fun with Karina. We took her shopping, went to the zoo and just had a great time. Grace fell in love with her. They would just sit in the cab together with the windows rolled and jump all over the place.

Yuro was continually making jokes, but he always new just what to do. He knew what to bring to the orphanage, what to bring the director, and how to schmooze her to get us in. He was a little like the Pied Piper. The last day when we were leaving we had a cook-out. All of the people who we had met helped us, and we had a big dish of pig fat and where drinking vodka. June was being encouraged to drink so I took her aside and said,

"June, throw it over your shoulder." So, that's just what she did and they were horrified that she would waste the vodka!

When we left we thought we were doing all right. We were trying to figure out what to do and Karina said, "I'll wait for you!" It was hard looking in the rear view mirror and seeing her just standing there in the parking lot.

When we got home we sent her letters and Barbie Dolls. Then the big 'kicker' came. They changed the law in Ukraine and we were no longer eligible to adopt Karina because of our age.

I have since heard from the agency that Karina was adopted, along with her siblings, which was great.

I have always felt that there was some reason I had gone there. I thought that she was my daughter. We were very attached to Karina but the most important thing is how she feels. What I mean, is that no matter how bad you feel, it's more important that the child you have left behind is not crushed in the process when they ask, "When are you coming back to take me away?"

In the back of my mind I am always thinking about Karina, and I am sure I always will."

After about eight days in Ukraine, Paula, Grace, June and Helene left the orphanage and made the journey home, bidding an emotional farewell to everyone that had touched them so deeply.

While the girls were in Ukraine, our dossier was still in process in Kiev and awaiting approval. So, even though we were disheartened about Karina, we waited on a decision being made in Kiev to see how we might move forward.

# The Invitation

Time passes slowly waiting for a referral for your child. We were used to this after so many failed attempts, so we ~~moved~~ continued on with our everyday lives, assuming that at some point we would get the call from the agency. We have depended upon our agency to be the guiding force behind the referral process and to make the machine move faster. This notion was insane, given that they have no connection or authority to the internal workings of the countries for which they work. Not their fault, just a fact.

*August 12th*
*Cleveland, Ohio*

On August 12th we received our appointment notification from the SDA in an email from the agency. It was short notice as we expected. Our appointment was set for September 8th in Kiev which was enough time to get the travel booked, arrange to get June to Cleveland again, buy new $100 bills, and generally put our plan into action.

My first call was to Aunt June. Aunt June has caller ID and said, "Hi Mike, I guess you're calling me because you got your appointment to go to Ukraine. When do I need to be there? I have to make arrangements for Rick and the dog."

"Well, what if try to get you up here a few days before we leave, say September 2nd? That way we will have time to make sure you are comfortable and the girls and Helene know the plan," I said.

"Okay, I'll be ready. Book the flight and call me."

Cindy, our travel agent, was next on the agenda with a quick email and a request for an open-end ticket*.

*TRAVEL NOTE: When booking your ticket, try to book your return flight later than you think you will need it. It is easier to change your ticket to come home earlier than to extend your flight. You will end up paying double change fees because you never really know exactly when you will be coming home until just a few days before you're ready to leave Ukraine.*

One of the more interesting issues you need to think about is currency. Most of the business you will be doing in Ukraine is in cash using U.S. currency. You will need to pay the facilitator, hotel, food, taxi, and everything else in cash. The law states that you can only have $10,000 per person entering Ukraine. Don't break this law as the local authorities can and will "relieve" you of any extra cash you are carrying. The best thing to do is split the cash with your spouse.

You will also need the best quality bills you can find. We visited our local bank and made a request for clean or new, $50 and $100 bills. Most banks take delivery of money once a week. In Ukraine, you can go to any bank to exchange your U.S. dollars but they will look at each bill and if there are any marks on them, including smudges or ink, they won't accept them.

For the next couple of weeks, I spent countless hours arranging my business affairs so that my clients were taken care of and making sure I had all of the documents and other items I would need to continue my consulting work without interruption while traveling. Also, at the top of my list was digitizing movies so Paula and I might have a little entertainment on the many nights we would spend in our tiny hotel room.

*[You can get pretty creative in this area with a little research into programs that will allow you to take commercial DVDs and make MP4 video files. You can also find great deals on 32 gig USB drives that can hold up to 30 movies.]*

Preparation is the key to normalcy on your journey. Try your best to keep a routine going. That will give you the edge you will need to get through the adoption process suffering only minor wounds. You will find the additional strength required to keep your cool and give up control (as you must) if you can get up each morning, have your coffee and go for a walk as usual. It will make everything a bit easier.

The days passed quickly. June arrived without incident, ready to return to motherhood and take on Grace and the parental responsibilities that would be required while we were away.

Everything was in order.

# The Journey Begins

*September 4th*
*Cleveland, Ohio*

On September 4th, Paula and I began our journey with open minds and open hearts. We had put the time in on multiple previous adoption attempts but this was somehow different. We thought for sure, that this time we would come back with a daughter and a sister for Grace. We knew it would be a long trip and were ready, but what we weren't ready for was the education and emotional rollercoaster.

Since Grace wasn't going with us, saying goodbye was not easy — but she was gracious and let us off the hook with a simple, "I love you Mama. Call me and write to me and bring me a sister – okay?" No time for tears.

June drove us to Cleveland Hopkins International Airport. She had agreed to return to Cleveland after the mission trip to Ukraine for Karina and stay with Grace for the extended time we would be gone. Little did she know how extended it would be.

Our itinerary was Cleveland to New York to Munich, Germany, arriving in Kiev, Ukraine two days later. It was not the best way to get there but with such short notice, it was the best that our travel agent could put together for us.

*September 5th*
*En route to Germany*

```
BLOG Entry - We are at a coffee shop on a
seven-hour layover in Munich. It's the
first time in all of our travels that
shopping abroad is not that much fun ...
the exchange is so poor for the U.S.
dollar that even the coffee seems like a
rip off ... $9 for two cups. We should
arrive today at 4 p.m. in Kiev where
hopefully we will meet a driver who will
take us to our apartment.


So far, our travel has been quite easy.
Lufthansa was great even though we were
packed in like sardines. We watched a
couple of movies, took a nap, and finally
arrived in Munich.
```

    We arrived in Munich with a seven-hour layover so we checked into the airport hotel and tried to get some sleep, which we did, like two rocks under a blanket. Not a sound and not a movement until the phone rang with our wake-up call a few hours later.

In two hours we were back on the plane and on our way to Kiev — a short three-hour flight. Arriving in Kiev, we had our first glance of the former USSR. Ukraine reminded us of a trip we took in 1997 to Moscow and St. Petersburg, Russia. The main difference was that Russia is recovering nicely from their turmoil, while Ukraine seems to be stuck in the 1950's. We could sense the poverty, lack of worldliness, and isolationism from which this country suffers.

After we collected our luggage and passed through passport control, we were to be met by the driver who had been set up by our facilitator. We headed in to the main lobby where a couple of hundred people stood waiting for friends and family along with hired drivers holding their signs. Our driver was not to be seen, so we stood still and waited in the center of the room hoping he might see us. Americans stick out like sore thumbs here. We look different — we look, well — American.

After about 30 minutes, we realized that we weren't going to get picked up by our driver and started looking for alternatives. Unfortunately, we could not think of many, since we could not speak a word of Russian and didn't not know a soul in this country. We tried to call Konstantin, our Ukrainian facilitator but didn't get through. We did, however, have the address of the apartment where we would be staying, and finding a driver who spoke enough English, we negotiated a fair price to take us into the city and to our apartment.

Kiev is a beautiful city — but it wasn't long before we realized we were in a very different place. Everything was different, different in a different way from China. We couldn't understand the signage or the people. We couldn't find a place to eat, a grocery store, coffee — you name it — we couldn't find it.

We were staying in an apartment close to Independence Square, which is the main tourist area next to an underground mall and probably the best luxury produce market on Mother Earth. I bought some cherries, and as good as they were, they were not worth the $28 per pound price tag. Just to make things clear, I was sure I was paying $2.80 — so much for my exchange rate calculations.

> **BLOG Entry** - Okay, folks. Today we meet with our facilitator (Konstantin for future reference). He is meeting us at our apartment. Nice place! Kind of reminds me of a low-end Jetsons pad with a TV that you can't understand.
>
> Our trip was long but fine ... did not sleep last night ... and according to my computer, it is 2:30 a.m. in Chagrin Falls. I took a long walk this morning in the city center to shoot some video and met a couple of kids who spoke English. They said that "Americans are good people but the USA and Ukrainian politicians are

making it difficult to remember that we
are all brothers and sisters ... God
created all of us." He has a point,
doesn't he?

Today, after we meet with Konstantin, we
are going to try to find a tour service
and explore the city and find something to
eat. This has been a challenge as most
Ukrainians eat meat, cookies and lots of
coffee!

Also, it is supposed to be very hot the
next couple of days (90°). Unfortunately,
I packed fall clothes, so this should be
interesting. Tonight or tomorrow, we
should have a better picture of the events
that will be coming our way and the
process we will undergo, so stay tuned ...

    Our apartment was interesting. Most, if not all, of the apartments are hidden inside some old dilapidated building (that could just as well be located in the slums of Harlem, New York) and require an entry code. We were told that once inside, we should lock the doors with all four deadbolts. A key operates the main door lock that you must turn four full revolutions engaging another heavy-duty pin.

Inside, the apartment was clean and was much like a small place in Manhattan with a kitchen and microwave, gas stove, and the bathroom with a combo washer/dryer. The living room was decorated with a small couch, a chair and a TV. There were no pictures on the walls, as Ukrainian people typically don't have extra money to spend on art.

This first apartment was equipped with an in-room A/C unit, which worked well and made sleeping in the small bed pretty comfortable. One of the things we were not ready for were the linens. In Ukraine, it is very rare to find a king or queen-sized bed, but most of the apartments have a queen. The odd thing is that the bottom sheet is a *full-size,* and not quite big enough to wrap around and tuck into the bed, so it just lies on top. The cover for the bed is typically a comforter with some kind of slipcover case, so it can get very, very warm.

After settling in, we ventured out to find water and food figuring that we would just eat something in the apartment and not try to figure out the restaurant system just yet. We found a small local market and had to put all our valuables into a locker before we entered. We wandered the aisles looking at lots of food we didn't recognize and decided to keep it simple. We bought yogurt, cheese, crackers, sardines, and water.

*TRAVEL NOTE: The water is mostly carbonated, mineral water that tastes very strange and slightly salty to foreigners, so we recommend buying the "Bon Aqua" brand. The un-carbonated version has a light blue cap, I think.*

The weather in Kiev is pleasant in September with sunny skies and temperature reaching into the seventies, so we took endless walks through the beautiful parks and did some general exploring.

*September 6th*
*Kiev, Ukraine*

```
BLOG Entry - Well, today we took it easy
and just walked, talked and shopped. The
weather has been really wonderful.
Hopefully, it will stay that way for
another couple of days.


Also, went to McDonald's instead of
Starbucks (my hang at home ... no Starbucks
here) at about 7 a.m.  They have terrific
coffee and it's cheap!  Made cup-by-cup,
fresh ground - sounds just like the way
they make their food - huh?


Paula and I probably walked 10 miles today
and took in the sights including the Opera
house and St Michael's Monastery, which was
built in 1108.  We actually witnessed an
```

```
Orthodox mass by the resident monks and a
wedding while we were there.
The architecture is awesome and inspiring.
Inside the monastery was even more so ...
(Paula and I were thinking of adding some
domes to the new patio deck we just
finished building...what do you think? :-)


I guess the big news is that tomorrow we
have an appointment with the SDA to meet
with the psychologists and pick a child. I
heard the step by step process from our
facilitator, Konstantin, and he says they
will show us three to five pictures of
young girls and Paula and I can talk about
them, ask questions and then - choose one.
That's it.  Amazing such a life changing
event and it all occurs in just a few
minutes.
```

As far as sightseeing in Kiev, you are largely limited to the monasteries and a few parks. You can easily spend two full days visiting them and learning about the Ukrainian people and their beliefs. Most, if not all, of the monasteries are open and fully operational with monks that live and work there. One of my favorites was Saint Michael's (of course!) The art and attention to detail were overwhelming, as was the sheer number of available worship opportunities. In one church, there were at least 15 confessionals with long lines of needy souls stretched along the walls. I was moved and in awe to be in such a place where you could feel the presence of Our Father.

On our third night in Kiev, we really had a craving for food other than the native Ukrainian cuisine that we still didn't quite understand, so we headed out in search of other international restaurant opportunities. We were unsuccessful because in Ukraine, and even in a city as large as Kiev, there are very few restaurants that cater to foreigners. I'll get into more detail about this later. We did, however, find one sushi restaurant where the food was fresh. It was also extremely expensive. If you figure that the exchange rate is four to one in our favor, and an average dinner in Kiev cost $10, $60 for sushi was through the roof!

# The State Department of Adoption Meeting

*September 8th*
*Kiev, Ukraine*

On our fourth day in Kiev, we were scheduled to have our referral meeting with the SDA [State Department of Adoption]. Both of us were very anxious — not knowing what would happen even though we had asked Konstantin repeatedly what the agenda would be.

The SDA is the formal federal agency that is responsible for the placement and oversight of all children for adoption in Ukraine. They are charged with keeping detailed records of the children, their status, history, medical conditions, etc. This is something they take very seriously, but do so without adequate technology and systems to be able to keep current, accurate records. The internal process of how the SDA works will unfold throughout our story. There is no one person to blame at the SDA when things go wrong — it's just that the system has not changed in 80 years.

On our first meeting with the SDA, we had no idea what to expect. I had envisioned Paula and I sitting on one side of a big desk and the three SDA interviewers in large chairs sitting on the other side looking down and grilling us. We thought we were very well prepared for all likely questions and I was dressed in what the agency told me to wear, a pair of khaki pants and sport coat. We were about to find out that we weren't as prepared as we thought.

We met Konstantin, our facilitator, who was dressed in a pair of jeans and a tee shirt with a light jacket, outside a small restaurant and walked the one-half mile through backstreets to the SDA office. It was a nice three-story building with a wonderful statue out front of a young woman holding a parasol.

Next to the office was a beautiful cathedral with golden domes, as is commonplace in Kiev. There was an unusual sign outside the SDA building in English: *"MINISTRY OF UKRAINE FOR FAMILY, YOUTH AND SPORTS."* This was the only sign in English we saw on our entire trip.

## The SDA

Inside, several couples were waiting for their appointments. An old guard was asleep on a couch. If you ever find yourself at the SDA, he will probably still be sitting there. He's easy to recognize because he is missing three fingers. After about 15 minutes, a 30-ish brunette woman summoned us upstairs and the butterflies started fluttering in my stomach.

The office was simply decorated with two desks, a couple of 1980s vintage computers and a small couch where we were directed to sit.

Introductions were very short …

"This is Michael and Paula Redman, etc., etc." and she said. "You are only eligible to adopt a child that is no more than 45 years younger than you." We did not expect to hear this so soon, but it did, in fact, confirm what we had heard on the blogs.

We sat, waiting for the grilling to begin as the SDA psychologist asked, "Why do you want to adopt this girl, and why in Ukraine?"

We answered, "We have come to Ukraine to adopt a child because we are fond of your country, and know there is a need for your children to have safe families and opportunity."

Then we sat waiting for the tough questions to come our way. They never did!

She turned around with her back to us and started leafing through her books of children that were available to us. Each book contained children of a specific age and I believe she was trying to find children that might fit our profile and that were healthy. We were looking for a girl and according to the new law she had to be 11-years-old. We were not happy about this but we were not going home without a child this time.

**BLOG Entry** - Paula and I had spent considerable time working on answers to specific questions, ("Why do you want to adopt in Ukraine? etc."), but when it went to "Would you tell me a little bit about your family?" the funny thing was we never thought of that question! Paula made a simple response; "there are four of us with son, Tyler, and daughter Grace…"

Next, the psychologist put one photo on the table - Konstantin looked, and talked with the interviewer, turned to us and said, "This is a girl of 10 years, healthy, etc." She looked very unhappy. We then were presented with three other photos. It was a little intense and intimidating because

```
the interviewer turned to us after the
third photo and said, "This is the perfect
child for you."  What do you say to that?


We asked for one more girl that was closer
to Grace's age … She pulled out another
photo.  "She has slight mental problems."
I took that as a clear sign that we were
done - PICK a girl now!! We took her word
on the perfect girl for us …
```

The first picture was put on the table.  Konstantin was handed a couple of papers that described the child, some legal disposition of her status and some notes from various people.  That continued until there were four children's pictures sitting in front of us.  We thought we would have some time to think about the children, ask questions and then get to talk to each other alone to decide which child to visit.  Wrong again…

The SDA person asked, "Which girl you would like to see?"  After a few minutes, we settled on a child named Emma.  She was cute, and the paperwork said she wanted to be adopted, got along well with adults, and was also a singer.  Our meeting was over 25 minutes after it started.  Nothing like we expected.

~ *The Next Step*

Typically, the SDA will create a referral document for the couple to meet the child. We were told we could pick up our papers to visit Emma in Donetsk the next day, so Paula and I left and went to a great little restaurant called Porto to celebrate. After a wonderful meal of Greek salad, shrimp scampi, and some very nice red wine, we walked back to the apartment.

*TRAVEL NOTE: On many restaurant menus, you will see a price and two measurements of volume. One is for the total weight of the meal and the other is a price that reflects [per 100 mg]. At Porto the salad was only $3 and the shrimp was $9 for just one shrimp! It was the head and tail but weighed about 100 mg. You can figure out the prices and portions of food pretty easily once you understand how the menus and weights work.*

# Donetsk, Ukraine

*September 9th*
*Donetsk, Ukraine*

The next morning, we walked to the SDA and picked up our referral papers, then scrambled off to have our dossier copied (all 200 pages, one at a time). The next order of business was to visit one of the local travel offices (they seem to be on every corner) to purchase two airline tickets for the following day to Donetsk, which is about 1,500 miles from Kiev. The total cost was around $450 and soon we headed back to our apartment to get packed and do a little last minute sightseeing.

*September 10th*
*Donetsk, Ukraine*

The next morning, after my customary search for coffee, Konstantin had his driver Sergio pick us up at the apartment and take us to the airport where he helped us with check-in. We were happy to pay him $50 for his services. (We later found out that you can get the same service for $20 by calling a local cab company.)

The flight to Donetsk was uneventful … and upon arrival, we met Vitaly for the first time. He would become our in-country guide, translator and friend for the next three-and-a-half weeks.  Vitaly is a well-educated, good-looking man, in his mid-40s with a reassuring smile, sideways sense of humor and definitely someone who takes care of business.

**Vitaly**

The Donetsk airport was my first experience with a Ukrainian public toilet and as I walked into the restroom, the stench was so strong I thought I might pass out.  I covered my nose with my shirt and went into an open stall.  There was a little hole cut in the concrete on the floor and nothing more.  I just wasn't ready for this in the year 2008 — on planet Earth — in a city the size of Donetsk. But then again, it could be normal on Mars.

We quickly loaded up and headed downtown in a cab. We soon met with a guy who rented apartments for roughly $80 per night at a place that resembled a war torn building from 1970 in Saigon, Vietnam.

Entering the apartment we noticed there was no bedroom, although there were two pull-out couches. There was no Internet as promised either. The man told us, "Internet access will be installed in the next couple of days and you will need to pay about $125 for installation", which I gladly said I was willing to do (feeling my wallet getting lighter by the second.) This turned out to be another scam and the more we talked to the owner the further out the installation date moved until it was almost two weeks away with no guarantee.

He also wanted us to pay for our entire stay, immediately. "You will need to pay me now for 30 days in advance. It is how we do our business here."

*TRAVEL NOTE: <u>Don't ever do that</u>. We found that at most places, you will only need to pay in advance for two to three days at a time. You will want to keep your commitment short because you never know what will happen next on your journey, or when you might need to travel somewhere else for papers or whatever on a moment's notice.*

After settling into our apartment and visiting a local grocery store for a few necessities, we headed to the regional inspector's office to check in and get permission to see Emma. Vitaly disappeared for 20 minutes and came out to tell us that we couldn't see Emma today because it was inconvenient for the inspector.

"Come back tomorrow," she said and I will take you to the orphanage along with the local KGB (the international security agency) representative.

The KGB has changed a bit since the old days of the USSR. Today, it is a formal organization that answers only to the president and does his bidding. They do not deal with the local authorities so everyone we met in Ukraine tries their best to stay as far away from the KGB as possible. Obviously, that part hasn't changed since the "old days."

```
BLOG Entry - We arrived in Donetsk and our adventure
    truly began.  First of all, we were told that it
    was too late for us to see Emma and that when we
    do get to see her, we need to be accompanied by
    the local supervisor and a Ukrainian official
    (former KGB agent) that will question Emma.
    This was new news to Vitaly, who is our guide
    and connection with the orphanage.  He said this
    is a new rule for this region that he just found
    out about.  We were disappointed, but tired from
    our trip, so seeing Emma the next day was fine
    with us.

    MR
```

We had some time on our hands so we wandered up the street and into downtown. Donetsk has a very nice town center (stay in the town center — it costs a bit more but your stay will be far more comfortable) and there were Internet Cafés everywhere. When you go into a café, just point at the clock and give them a pencil and paper. They will tell you how much in Hryvnia (pronounced greev-na) per hour it costs to use a computer. At the time of our visit we saw the exchange rate go from 4 to 1 U.S., all the way up to 9 to 1 U.S.

In the middle of the Donetsk town center was our first introduction to what I call the 'Lenin Phenomenon.' His statue is everywhere in Ukraine despite the fact that most Ukrainians hate him. We believed it was because it was better to have a statue of Lenin than no statues at all and that the communists who still live there use the statues of Lenin as a gathering place to celebrate important events. The town center also had a beautiful fountain surrounded by a few restaurants and shops. It was a shame we didn't get to spend more time in Donetsk, as it seemed like an extraordinary little city.

**Donetsk**

To wrap up our first day in Donetsk, we went to Vitaly's apartment and were absolutely shocked that the rental guy would let anyone see, let alone stay in a place like this. It was a one-room apartment in a bad section of town, on the 10th floor. Doesn't sound that bad, but I was scared that we would die in the elevator on the way up as it creaked so badly and the cables whined.

Once in the apartment, I told Vitaly, "You can't stay here. It's just too awful. There are bugs everywhere. It's filthy and there's no hot water!" I mean this place was scary.

Vitaly told us that it would be "Okay" and we should not worry about him. That was my first real insight into his world.

Dinner in a local restaurant, and sleep followed.

*September 11th*
*Donetsk, Ukraine*

I woke up bright and early and walked to a nearby hotel to use their Internet and get some coffee which was a very good European blend — much like espresso. (I later found out that 99 percent of the coffee in Ukraine is manufactured by the American company, Nescafe.) I have to say that I was really growing fond of their coffee. My poor attempt at ordering coffee was funny, waving my hands, pointing at cups, no milk, no sugar ... the waiter didn't understand a word I was saying, but I was lucky and his guess was much better than my gestures.

Next, I spent an hour talking online with my programmers at work in Russia and the U.S. to keep my business on track. Then back to the apartment to see Paula and hopefully get to meet Emma later in the morning. When I arrived at the apartment, Paula was having some tea. I grabbed some crackers and our last can of sardines when the phone rang.

"I am outside. Let's go meet Emma now," Vitaly said. It was 10 a.m. and he told us that we needed to pick up the inspector and then we'd go to the orphanage. I had envisioned the inspector as a 50ish tough Communist leftover, since she was able to blow Vitaly off so easily the day before. Five minutes later we got another call that she would meet us at the orphanage. So off we went, full of anticipation and excitement to meet our new daughter.

I was a little surprised when we pulled up to a well kept building that appeared to be a boarding school and not an orphanage, but Vitaly told me, "Many orphanages in the bigger cities are nice and some local children come here to just go to school and are not orphans at all."

### *There are four reasons children end up in orphanages in Ukraine.*

1. *They are truly orphans and have no parents or relatives.*

2. *Their parents have lost their custody privileges, typically due to physical, alcohol, or other substance abuse (many of these children have siblings and other family members who are unable to support them).*

3. *A parent cannot afford to keep a child because of their economic state.*

4. *They live near the orphanage and attend school.*

After a bit of verbal wrangling to find someone in charge, we were taken to a classroom on the second floor and after making ourselves comfortable, the inspector came in. She was nothing like I imagined. She was about 25 years-old, very attractive and very talkative. It's Ukraine after all and you never know what to expect! We exchanged a few words, and then were told Emma was on her way. The three of us sat and waited ... the anticipation was a bit overwhelming.

"What will she be like?" Paula asks, "Where should we sit? You sit there and she can sit between us."

**Paula and Vitaly waiting for Emma**

Emma finally walked through the door and was taller than I had imagined. Emma looked more like 14 than an 11-year-old and she was so unhappy. She sat down right across from Paula and I who were smiling away, but she was not. The orphanage director and Vitaly were speaking to her in Russian for what seemed like an hour but was probably more like two minutes.

Then, Emma spoke through Vitaly, "I do not want to be adopted by anybody. Now can I go back to my room?" It was not exactly what we expected her to say, nor what we wanted to hear. The meeting was over!

That's just how quick it can happen. We were in shock, but as the story unfolded we learned more. Emma didn't even know we were coming until we were waiting for her in the classroom. She also had relatives we were not told about by the SDA. The call that was made to the orphanage while we were having our SDA referral meeting was to someone who lied and Konstantin didn't follow up with anyone to confirm anything we were hearing. Paula and I were starting to understand that everything was not as it appeared. Some people in the Ukraine adoption system will give you incomplete or wrong information, and then point the finger at someone else with no accountability. This type of thing happened time and time again.

> **BLOG Entry** - Apparently, Emma was not interested in being adopted. She has a grandmother and younger sister nearby and she thinks that her parents will get it together to come and get her out of the orphanage. We are disappointed, but as the Assistant Director said, "Life goes on."

```
But, wouldn't it be nice if the orphanages all
had Skype and we could have done that interview
without the expense and time involved with
travel?
```

We walked out of the Donetsk orphanage more than a bit confused, but understanding that Emma was a nice girl who was just not ready to be adopted. Vitaly, called Konstantin who told us, "This had never happened before," and we would need to petition for another meeting with the SDA. Boy, was that a stretch ... we found out on our trip that this is a very regular occurrence, and that the older children have first say when it comes to *who* and *if* they want to be adopted.

We needed to go back to Kiev, file another petition for an SDA meeting, and then start the entire process over. This didn't bother us too much as we thought it was just a mistake and not systemic. We sure were glad that we had not paid for 30 days at that apartment!

After lunch, Vitaly jumped into action and booked us a flight back to Kiev for the next morning. Back to the apartment, pack up, a quick bite for dinner and hit the sack.

*TRAVEL NOTE: This little side trip to Donetsk added 10 days to our trip and cost just over $2,500 for flights, hotel and expenses. This is to be expected with an adoption in Ukraine. The process is fluid and you are not in control. I will repeat this little message over and over throughout this book so hopefully it will sink in...*

# SDA Second Meeting

*September 12th*
*Kiev, Ukraine*

The very next morning we drove to the Donetsk Airport and after a brief flight, arrived back in Kiev. Again we were met by Konstantin's driver, Andrei, who took us to another apartment in Kiev, which was in more of a neighborhood setting and a 30-minute walk from Independence Square. This can make a difference for dining, shopping, and your general comfort. The apartment was on the 7th floor, spacious, had Internet and we were happy enough just to be there.

*September 13th*
*Kiev, Ukraine*

```
BLOG Entry - Hi All,
Well, today we are hoping to hear from the SDA
that we can meet with them again, and start
all over.  Konstantin is at the SDA ... boy
are we learning patience the hard way :)
```

Unfortunately, the weather in Kiev over the past five days had gone downhill and it was very cold, windy and raining. *It stayed that way until we left.*

So let's see.  It was Saturday and we had submitted our second SDA petition.  Konstantin had assured us that they would give us a very quick meeting because they were embarrassed that Emma didn't want to be adopted and had made a mistake.

We spent the next few days just waiting and spending $130 a night at an apartment near the U.S. Embassy. There was not much to do because we weren't close to any of the typical tourist activities or restaurants.  Our diet for those few days consisted mostly of our yogurt, crackers, and some sardines. Sound familiar?  Not too appetizing but it worked.

One of the more incredible attractions in Kiev was the Opera House, which has performances seven nights a week. Each night there is a different show and general admission is as low as $6.  Paula and I went for the big bucks seats at $35 and sat dead center in row H.  The show was *Zorba the Greek*, performed flawlessly by a cast of over 100 with a full orchestra.

In my past life, I made my living composing and producing music for many years and I can tell you that I haven't heard many orchestras of this caliber anywhere.  If you get the chance, please don't pass up the Kiev Opera.

**The Kiev Opera House**

**BLOG Entry** - Last night we went to the ballet at the Opera house and saw "Zorba the Greek". Walked home afterward as you do everywhere here. Reminds me of walking with Jeff McElnea in New York when I was working on Adjacket. Jeff could walk sooooo fast ... Getting in shape while we are not doing anything else here is a plus.

Finally, Konstantin called and said we have another meeting with the SDA on the following Tuesday, but then we received another call from Konstantin telling us that he had to travel out of town and his associate George would meet us. We weren't concerned at this point but we should have been.

*\*\* Please read this next paragraph very carefully. \*\**

When we arrived at the SDA for our second referral meeting, we met George who was a friendly, tall man with an engaging smile. He exuded confidence and was very reassuring as he said, "What happened to you could never happen again. A bullet never lands in the same place two times."

I could spend a lot of time telling you about our second meeting with the SDA but nothing was different from the first meeting with the exception of one thing. We were expecting an apology, or some concern on the part of the psychologist but she didn't even look at us. This was when I began to get nervous.

At the end of our 20-minute meeting, we had chosen a child named Julia in a small town called Melitopol, which is some 400 miles southwest of Kiev. We asked for more information and were told, "She wants to be adopted. She is a nice girl, smart and quiet, and has no medical conditions." That was almost enough for us but I wanted George to call the orphanage and talk to the director. He tried to talk to him but was told he was busy and to call back in the morning.

We felt pretty good about this referral, but I still needed some confirmation that Julia truly wanted to be adopted and I just couldn't stop thinking about it.

The next morning we were told that our referral was ready and that we could come pick it up. When we met George, he was ready to get us on the train to Melitopol where Julia's orphanage was located. I asked him if he had talked to the director and he said, "The director called me and said everything is fine." That was not enough for me though, and I asked George to call him back while we were there. He had no trouble getting Valery, the orphanage director, on the phone and was quickly told, "Julia is a very nice girl. She sings and won our karaoke contest and she wants to be adopted."

After the call, George turned to us with his big smile and cavalierly said, "You see, everything is fine and you will have a nice little girl. Do not worry." We had been told this before and were hopeful but by no means, convinced.

We finally said okay and George took us to the train station. We didn't know at this point that the most important thing to understand about your adoption in Ukraine is ***you get a maximum of two referrals — period.*** Had we known this fact, and had Konstantin been present at the second referral, and had we known then that it was our last shot … we would have preceded very differently.

# Melitopol, Ukraine

Paula and I had heard mixed reviews about travel by train in Ukraine and Paula was quite nervous, but we didn't have a choice, as there was no airport in Melitopol.

As it turned out, first-class travel on the train was not very expensive and was in fact, comfortable. We had two, seat-type beds and the restroom was at the end of the hall. We didn't have running water (because I didn't know how to turn it on), but that wasn't too bad, even though it was a 12-hour trip from Kiev to Melitopol.

*TRAVEL NOTE: For reference, don't take less than second-class on a train. Second-class has four beds and you have to buy all of them if you want any privacy. After second-class, you will be in the cattle car.*

We settled into our compartment and made ourselves as comfortable as possible — stuffing our bags under the small beds on each side. We sat around for a while reading and chatting about our ever-changing adoption plan and wondering what Melitopol would be like, especially since it was such a small dot on the Ukraine map. At about 10 p.m. we killed the lights and tried to go to sleep. That's when they turned the heat on. Our compartment turned into a small furnace within 20 minutes with the temperature hitting 90°F!

After a little investigation, we discovered, unfortunately, that the heating coils were under the bed with no way to turn them off. No luck sleeping tonight.

**Typical First-Class train compartment**

Upon our 5:30 a.m. arrival in Melitopol we were exhausted, but as we exited the train, Vitaly was standing there to welcome us and direct us to a waiting taxi. The driver's name was Sasha and he would spend the next three weeks driving us. We made quick friends with Sasha and he was always on call to take us anywhere we needed to go… to and from the orphanage, to restaurants, and around town to file papers. When we needed to go to Zaporizhzhya to get documents notarized, his brother drove us.

TRAVEL NOTE: *Once you have reached your destination, it is a good idea to form a relationship with a driver. Taxis will try to overcharge you, so having a driver can save you money. If you must take a regular taxi, make sure you have a firm price set first — otherwise you may be paying a multiple of what the fair price should be.*

Melitopol was a small, sprawling city with a population of roughly 100,000, and as we drove through town from the train station we could see and feel the poverty. The homes were very small and run down, people walked the streets pushing old grocery carts, and every pothole we hit was so deep they made my stomach lurch.

I was so hungry I couldn't help but keep asking Vitaly to find us a place to eat before we looked for a place to stay, but he had never been to Melitopol either. It was also very early and nothing was open but we did manage to find a restaurant with a small buffet. Upon entering, we noticed that the workers were all wearing these funny little white hats made out of paper. It was the uniform here. The food in the line didn't look at all familiar to me and what we ultimately ordered was some kind fish salad held together with mayonnaise. It was a new taste — unusual — but at least it stopped the rumbling in my stomach. It scared us to think that we might have to eat this type of food for the next month. Paula was contemplating an extended fast.

The weather was mild and sunny when but quickly deteriorated into a grey, cold, rainy day and made us feel right at home — just like we had never left Cleveland. The Melitopol Hotel, which was the first place we stopped on our search for accommodations, was pretty interesting in that it was a casino, a rundown hotel, and probably also a brothel.  They wanted $140 a night for a room with a single bed, no clean sheets, no toilet, and a bath with no shower.  We decided that there must be a better place.  There was.

After a few phone calls, Vitaly was able to find us a nice little hotel for $60 a night that included breakfast and free laundry service but no Internet.  The two women that ran the hotel as part of a textile company were very accommodating and tried their best to take care of us.  Unfortunately, with all the bad weather and daily half-mile trek to find an Internet connection, we only stayed five days before finding another hotel closer to the city center, which was more expensive but did have wireless Internet, our only connection to Grace, home and work.

We weren't in Melitopol for more than a couple of hours and Vitaly was already hard at work, contacting the regional inspector Svetlana and trying to make arrangements to visit the orphanage.  She said, by law, she would need to accompany us on every visit to the orphanage and she must ask us some questions, so we called Sasha to drive us to her office.  Svetlana was very dry and official and her questions, endless … why we were here? Why did we want to adopt from Ukraine? And on and on.

*It's a good idea to have your answers prepared for stock questions prior to travel if for no other reason than to reduce your stress level.*

After about 30 minutes with Svetlana, she was satisfied that we were not going to torture the children and told us we could pick her up at her office in the morning to visit Julia.

*September 15th*
*Novomykolaivka, Ukraine*

At 9 a.m. sharp, Sasha was at the door of the Seven Stars Hotel with Vitaly. We stopped and picked up Svetlana as we headed out of town.

The drive to the orphanage took 30 minutes through lush farmland and deep into the rural countryside. It was immediately obvious why the vegetables here have such an incredibly rich flavor and are generally the size of what we might call 'Nuclear Veggies.' The earth was dark brown, almost black from decades of decaying sunflower seeds. Farmers can't afford fertilizer or pesticides, so all of the food produced in Ukraine is naturally organic. I heard a story from a young lady describing in detail how, during WWII, the occupying Germans commandeered local citizens to shovel dirt into freight trains and transport it all the way back to Hitler in Germany. Now that's good dirt!

As we approached the small village of Novomykolaivka, home to the orphanage, we came to a quick and unplanned stop. Sasha pointed down the hill in front of us where there was one lone farmer ushering a small herd of cattle towards us taking over the entire road. It was obvious who had the right of way, so we just waited as they passed on both sides of our car … it was a very funny moment as the cattle poked their heads into the car to check us out.

We entered the main gates of the orphanage that consisted of a collection of rundown one to three-story buildings, nestled among a farm equipment, a repair shop and what I think must have been a goat farm. When we pulled in. there were children milling about but nobody really seemed to notice us. We were soon ushered to the director's office.

Valery, the director, was a thick man with a big smile (although we didn't see it on our first visit), in his mid 60s. His one word of English was "Okay," which was one more word than I knew in Russian. He began by asking Vitaly a slew of questions as Paula and I waited in silence.

**Valery and Paula**

After a few minutes, Julia appeared in the doorway with her teacher. She was small, and looked a bit unhappy, but curious. She sat next to Vitaly and checked us out, but wouldn't talk to anybody. I thought to myself, "This is not the winner of a karaoke contest that Valery told George about on the phone." Vitaly, Valery, and a teacher tried to get Julia to speak to us, but she was content to just sit still and have us talk. She appeared to be trying to smile and we thought it was going to be okay.

**Paula and Julia M**

Talking through Vitaly, we asked Julia some questions but her response was a faraway stare and an occasional "Da." Having never been through something like this, we didn't know what to expect and were just happy not to get shut down like we were when we met Emma. Paula and I exchanged looks of concern but also an, "Oh well, let's see where this goes."

Valery then proudly took us on a small tour of the orphanage that was eye-opening, because I had never been to an orphanage before and had no idea what to expect. A group of 12 children gathered as we walked outside but then Valery said a couple of words in his booming voice and they all disappeared in a flash.

The first thing I noticed was how the girls slept 15 to a room with no pictures on the walls, the windows didn't open and the absence of any decor. The beds were perfectly made with matching bedspreads and their shoes placed neatly by the foot of each bed. Each girl had a small locker for her personal belongings but no lock, which kind of defeated the purpose of having a locker. The washrooms had a single low profile [six inches off the floor] tub and four sinks. We were told that the girls took a bath once a week and most of the time without hot water. I couldn't imagine someone dumping cold water on you when it is 10 degrees outside.

**The Girls Dorm**

The boys' rooms, although neat, smelled of urine, and we were told that it really didn't bother them much. They live a little bit like wild animals, with minimal supervision outside of the structured school hours.

One of the last stops on our tour was a cool little room that housed the school's museum. There was a small plow from the turn of the century that used here at the orphanage, an old phonograph that Valery told me was his as a boy when he listened to classical music 10 hours a day and many photo books. Valery showed me his high school picture … he was a very handsome young man.

After our tour we were taken to the orphanage's performance hall, a small narrow room with stark white walls and about 80 seats. It was set up like a theater with a small stage, a boom box with the children waiting for us to arrive. They stared and smiled at us as we were seated in the front row.

All of the sudden the boom box roared … and we realized that the children were going to put on a show for us. One by one, groups of about five children stood up and sang karaoke, danced, or both. Paula looked at me and whispered, "Look at their faces. It's like they're saying, 'Look at me! Don't you want me to be your son or daughter?'" It was not sad, but very entertaining as almost every child performed. After each song the room erupted in applause. The children were so supportive of each other.

While we were watching the show, one little girl stood out and we later found that she was the true karaoke champ Valery had mentioned in his description of Julia when we called earlier. Her name was Nadya, a very cute little girl with blonde hair and an infectious giggly smile. She kept looking at Paula and singing directly to her, eye to eye. Later , when we stopped by one of the teacher's classrooms, the kids were watching soap operas on television and Nadya just sat there again, staring at Paula.

Overall, we felt that the first day went well with the inspector, the director and Julia. We were starting to think things just might work out for us this time. We also learned that we were the first American couple to adopt from this orphanage in its 80 years of operation. I expect the reason was their remote location. It also meant that the children and the staff didn't really understand why we were at the orphanage in the first place and as we would soon find out, nobody knew how to complete the mountains of adoption paperwork required by the Ukrainian government.

It had been a long and emotional day and we were once again ready for a good meal. The woman running the front desk at Seven Stars recommended a restaurant called "Classic" that would soon become one of the very few places we would regularly eat on our journey. One of the greatest things about Classic was their English menu, sort of … We still had to use our newly acquired cheat sheet supplied by Vitaly and it was also helpful that one of the servers [Anna] was attending the local University studying English.

It was a brisk night and the twenty-minute walk to the restaurant was refreshing. It gave us time to reflect on the day's events, reconnect with one another and let down our defenses, if even for a short while. Each night, when we took this walk to Classic we tried a different route until we were sure we had the shortest way home after dinner. We had always felt safe here, but you wouldn't want to expose yourself to the unnecessary risk of walking in the wrong area at the wrong time.

When we arrived at the restaurant, we sat in the main dining area, which was separate from the hipper dining room with live entertainment. Live entertainment in Ukraine usually consisted of a DJ that might be playing an instrument, or not, and sings — or not.

There was one table with a white tablecloth, that was to become "our table," by a window and a few feet from a birdhouse filled with happy little chirping birds. As with every restaurant we visited, the 42-inch flat-screen TV blared the latest pop music videos.

Our favorite meal consisted of the most wonderful Mediterranean salad with pine nuts, borscht or pea soup, a chicken cutlet or Ukrainian omelet with spinach, and 100 ml of their Nemiroff Pepper Vodka.

*September 16th*
*Melitopol, Ukraine*

Bright and early we are headed out to visit Julia and the local inspector Svetlana informed us that she would no longer need to accompany us to the orphanage. We could only think that she now trusted us and we were there to help the children. We never saw her again.

Julia met us as we pulled in and we asked the director if we could take her shopping in Melitopol to see if we might be able to get through to her. He agreed to allow us to do this even though it is against prevailing Ukrainian orphanage rules of which he is the regional director. I guessed that he had been watching our interaction with all of his children and knew we weren't a threat. We asked Julia if she would like to bring a friend, feeling that it would make her feel more comfortable and she has decided to bring her best friend, Albina.

*When we first met Albina, it was on a short tour of the school. Paula and I were standing in one of the classrooms and this young woman comes running up to me and smiling widely, says, "Spoon - Fork – Knife!" I looked over at Paula and there was another little girl named Nadya reading to her from an English book.*

Albina was a bubbly, sweet young lady that reminded both Paula and I of Julia Roberts. If she had a daughter, she would look exactly like Albina.

**Julia M, Albina, Paula and Me**

Back to Melitopol we went, with Sasha at the wheel to go shopping, not saying a word, but listening to the two girls talk nonstop. Paula and I just sat there and from time to time asked Vitaly, "What are they saying? Are they talking about us?"

Most of the time he would reply, "They are just talking about Ukrainian things." Of course, you always imagine that they are talking about you, how funny Americans speak, etc.

The girls spoke Russian as most people in Ukraine do except for the eastern provinces, which still maintain the native Ukrainian language. Paula and I tried to learn as many Russian words as we could but we found the sounds hard, and we were tongue-tied a lot.

Vitaly took us to a store called AMC TOP where we were shocked once again. It was modern and very large with just about anything you might need, but with a focus on food. I don't think the girls had ever seen anything like this western-style Wal-Mart store before and as soon as we walked in, Albina's eyes widened and Julia seemed to perk right up.

The trip to the store was to pick up a few essentials for the girls and maybe a couple of small gifts, but it soon turned into a shopping frenzy. Julia would pick up something, look it over very carefully and put it back on the shelf. Albina on the other hand would look at the item, look at us, and if we weren't looking, put it in the basket. It was really funny to watch them on what was probably their first shopping experience.

**BLOG Entry** - Hi everybody,

Sorry we have not updated the blog in a few days but our life has been a bit upside down and full of wait ... wait ... wait :)But finally, we have something to talk about!

```
On our second meeting at the SDA, we
received a referral in Melitopol ... a
small town (village) in southern Ukraine.
We left our utopia in Kiev and traveled by
train to Melitopol.


Julia M is quiet and shy.  We are hopeful
to make her part of our family ... More to
come...


Oh - one last thing - Julia's best friend,
Albina, is a beaming little girl who is
full of energy.  If we can figure out how
to do it, we'd love to take her home with
us too.
Thanks for following ... Michael
```

*September 17th*
*Melitopol, Ukraine*

Our second meeting with the director Valery was very interesting indeed. We were invited into his office with Vitaly and he asked that I sit next to him. His office was very small with windows and a view of the street so he could see everyone who was coming and going. After the usual greetings, Valery set about the ritual of offering us a spread of fruit, cheese, candy, little cakes, coffee, and chia (tea). Last, but not least, cognac.

Yep, it was 11 a.m. and true to reputation, the drinking hour starts when you wake up here. Not wanting to offend Valery, I reluctantly said, "okay," knowing full well that I would probably be struggling to stay awake later. Paula and I are not drinkers and a glass of wine is just fine for us.

Valery opened his private little cabinet that was adorned inside with various bottles of cognac, and vodka. He pulled out two shot glasses and then his own special measuring glass from his jacket pocket. We then had a little cheese and he pours very well measured shots for the two of us.

I do not know how, but Vitaly got out of it. I think he told Valery, "I have a heart condition so I cannot drink," which Valery accepted. We raise our glasses and drank… the burn starting slowly in my throat and dropping to the pit of my stomach as I gasp for breath. Paula is speechless, and Valery makes a painful grimace. Then we all laugh … how crazy is that?

Before I can even recover, Valery looks at me, smiles and pours another, and then another. Suddenly I feel more open, friendly and happier to be in Ukraine. The cognac is working its evil magic. We talk about life and Valery's past which was riveting given that he started working at the orphanage when he was eighteen.

Valery graduated college with a degree in music, with trumpet as his primary instrument. It is unclear how he ended up at the orphanage but he has been here exactly 50 years. He is a warm, complicated man and a great host. The children like and respect him and I truly believe that he really wants what is best for them. You have to realize that these children have been sheltered from the real world and Valery has grown up in the same environment.

An hour after sitting down with Valery we are having a wonderful time trying to understand each other and finishing off his bottle of cognac. Paula was smarter than me, as she usually is, and stopped after her third shot. I, on the other hand, am trying to be the diplomat and keep up with Valery — mistake. This is his country and obviously one of his favorite pastimes. My head is slightly spinning, and it is only 1 p.m. I figured that I would be able to go back to the hotel and take a nap, but it's not going to happen. Valery has other plans for us.

We finally stood to say goodbye and Valery says, "Michael, Paula, please stay for dinner and disco. I would like to have you as my guests here tonight. Come and I will show you the guest room."

Paula and I exchange quick looks. She could see in my eyes that I am not ready for this. It is a very nice offer, but not today. Valery leads us down the hall, unlocks a door and we enter a very nice room with multiple beds and a clean western bathroom.

"This is where our childrens' parents and guests stay when they come to visit us."

As nice as it was, we wanted to sleep in our own beds — especially after the cognac.

"Valery, thank you very much for the invitation, maybe another night."

"You must stay for disco, the children are counting on it."

As you see, now we do not have a choice … how can we disappoint the kids? They have nothing and we are so special to them, if only as a curiosity, so we agree.

I am not sure how I'm going to make it through the rest of the day, but we're walking to a little store down the street with a couple of the boys to buy them ice cream, then to stroll around the dirt roads in the village.

Dinner that night was with the children in the cafeteria. It consisted of soup, some kind of pasta hash and bread with lard to spread on it. I ate very little and Paula fasted. Valery had disappeared by this point and I suspected he had had as much fun as he could stand and gone home — leaving us to entertain, and be entertained, by the kids.

Around seven o'clock, Nika brought the boom box over to the main residence and set it up as we were playing ping-pong. It was simply amazing how quickly the kids were learning. The first day of ping-pong I looked like a champ and now I was just the guy who *used to be the champ* … as it is most times in life.

Promptly at 7:30, the room filled with about 50 children. It was already dark outside and Nika turned the music up almost to the point of distortion — not past — but right on the verge of turning into fuzz.

We danced… and danced… and danced.

It was a true mini-disco that was conducted here every Saturday night. Paula and I danced until we thought our feet might fall off. It was hot and sweaty, but the energy level was through the roof as kids jumped up and down, did flips and spun on the floor. I remember one special dance with a young woman named Sveta. She held my hands tightly and stared at me the whole time. I could tell that it meant a lot to her and she felt special. I did too. All of the children were lining up to dance with us, not because we were good dancers but because we were adults, power figures taking a personal interest in them.

Somewhere around 9 o'clock, we had Sasha pick us up and take us back to Melitopol, to Seven Stars and our own comfortable bed.

*September 18th*
*Melitopol, Ukraine*

All in all things, were going pretty well until went to pick up Julia at the orphanage in the morning. She had fallen back in a deep funk. Paula, Vitaly and I talked a lot about this and finally decided to call the inspector and have a local psychologist meet with her to see what was going on — which he did the next day. The doctor reported that she was just fine, a little confused and she would be all right if we would give her some time. All the while, we were getting pressure from Konstantin to close the deal, accept her and get the paperwork back to the SDA in Kiev as soon as possible.

"Well, I hope she turns around. This is scary. What if we get her home and she falls apart?" Paula said that night.

"Yeah, I know what you mean. It could be a train wreck. We'll just have to give it a couple of days and see where this all leads." I said, not very convincingly.

The fact was that both of us were uncomfortable with the situation and Julia's attitude. You know how you get those gut feelings and sometimes don't act on them only to regret it later. Well, that's how I was feeling and neither of us slept well.

*September 19th*
*Melitopol, Ukraine*

I was up early, took my usual walk and Sasha picked us up to head out to the orphanage again. It was particularly beautiful with the sun finally breaking through the grey sky in Melitopol. There were maybe a dozen farmers on the side of the road selling their produce right out of the fields, and the rich earth stretched out for miles. The thirty-minute trip seemed to get shorter every day, but you would always know when you arrived in the village because of the hundreds of huge black birds that lined the road, cattle roaming aimlessly, rusty 1930s bicycles and an occasional vintage motorcycle streaming past on their way to nowhere.

The village of Novomykolaivka is small with only about 10 farms, the orphanage, a building that housed the post office, mayor and police, and an old one story, 15-room hospital. I imagine the population to be about 200, not including the orphanage.

As always, 30 smiling children would run to our car as we approached the main entrance to their dormitory to greet us. They wanted to touch us, to touch the inside of Sasha's cab and just be close to us. We are potential parents, a ticket out of this place, and hopefully they see us as two people who care about them. Dogs and cats are everywhere, some with names and some without, but each one is taken care of by the children. They sneak food to them and in return, receive affection, which is something they are lacking.

Over time, Paula and I were getting close to the kids, seeing more in their eyes, more in their hearts. Each one had a story, an education for us westerners. Life was hard for them and hard for us to understand. There was a little boy I liked a lot who I nicknamed King Arthur [he had a shaved head.] He would follow me, stand on my right side and grab my hand, which he would gently put around his shoulder. King Arthur never said a word to me in all the time we visited but I felt his presence deeply, and his desire of the comfort of just being close to me.

**King Arthur and Me**

Then there was Vaughn, a good-looking, 13-year-old boy who followed us everywhere. He never spoke either, but was in every picture with his gentle smile. You could tell he was kindhearted and would have made any parent proud.

**Nick and Vaughn**

I could go on and on telling you about each of the children and how special all of them were, but you will find out for yourself if you ever visit an orphanage in person. If you do, I would encourage you to give your heart freely to these kids.

**Our Kids**

I am sure you have heard many stories about the children in Russian and Ukrainian orphanages having all sorts of disorders, but here in Melitopal most of the children are healthy and suffer only from the emotional wounds associated with a hard childhood. They are a family, a single, ever-changing family that plays, works and studies together. Every one of them wants what every other child wants and deserves — a mom, a dad and a future.

Finally, Julia came out of her dorm to meet us and to our surprise she seemed to have snapped out of her bad mood from the previous day and was trying to communicate with us. She was smiling and happy. We walked around the orphanage grounds, spending time with her and the other children. At the end of the day, Paula and I decided to move forward with the paperwork and the SDA, even though we were still nervous and felt that something still was not right.

We also asked Valery if we could take Julia out for the weekend, bringing her back in the evenings. He agreed.

*September 20th*
*Melitopol, Ukraine*

When we arrived at the 'internot' [the local term for an orphanage] around 11 a.m. the children were everywhere playing, running and chasing the dogs. Julia was not to be found. We asked around and when we finally found her, she didn't seem to have the slightest interest in going into town with us. We loaded into the car and she wouldn't look at us for the entire trip into town.

I thought, "Here we go again." and boy, was I right. The next two days were really tough. Julia retreated into her shell, cried, and basically shut down. She was totally beyond our reach … we felt so bad for her, but couldn't connect at all. It was now obvious to us that Julia didn't want to be adopted. Later we would find out there was much more to her story.

Sunday was City Day in Melitopol, which is a day of celebration and dedicated to all of the residents. Melitopol had decorated the streets and set up a huge stage right in front of our hotel. It was wild because there would be a booth serving vodka, next to one showing off the latest electrical generators, next to one doing a live runway show modeling nightgowns. Vitaly, Paula, Julia and I spent the day walking down Main Street visiting the various booths that offered food or some type of business service.

Julia didn't participate in any way, but tagged along and generally put up with us. I felt kind of stupid because I was going out of my way to entertain her and she just looked at us like we were crazy people. Day turned into night, and we were still walking the streets. By 7:30, our feet had had enough. We drove Julia back to the internot in silence and retreated to the comfort of Seven Stars, where we could view the festivities and listen to a band playing Led Zeppelin on the stage from the comfort of our room.

We were told they would be shooting fireworks at 9:00, so I left Paula in the room and wandered out onto the street. The crowd was 50 deep waiting for the finale to a long day of celebration, and then it happened. I had my video camera pointed at the sky to catch the action when just fifteen feet from me the rockets started blasting off—- boom, boom at a decibel level that shocked my system to the core. The guy next to me was screaming at the top of his lungs, jumping up and down, music blared and the show was underway.

After a few minutes of mayhem, I worked up the nerve [or stupidity] to move closer to the source of the blasts because I had never been this close to fireworks. Standing five feet or so away from the rocket tubes, I experienced a feeling I will never forget or have again. Sensory overload is the best way I can explain it. The rockets make an eerie thudding sound when they shoot and the deeper the thud, the bigger the explosion in the sky. At the end of the display, there were hundreds of simultaneous thuds shooting rockets skyward, a blur of street shaking explosions, and the hotel danced in the sunlight of night turned to day.

\* *We later found out from Nika that Julia M had siblings and a grandmother that regularly visited her but nobody had told us and the information was not listed in the SDA reports. She was also hoping that her parents would take her back. This type of thing happens all the time in Ukraine, and it's another reason you need to be very careful when you accept an SDA referral. We have heard that it is possible to make referral stipulations with the SDA that may help you with regards to the two-referral law.*

*September 21st*
*Melitopol, Ukraine*

Today was my birthday, which was a non-event as it has been so much of my life. Not that I really care, given that we were in Ukraine on an adventure. It's only a small blip on our journey and I was happy to get a couple of emails from friends and family wishing me well.

Later in the evening, having spent the weekend in misery, and watching Julia suffer as well, I carefully approached Paula and asked, "What do you think is going on with Julia? I am not sure this is the right thing to do. It's really making me uncomfortable," and I wait for a response… finally it came…

"I feel exactly the same. We have made a terrible mistake. We should never have agreed to accept Julia's referral. We both knew something wasn't right. What are we going to do now?"

Within five minutes I was on the phone with Vitaly. "Vitaly, I know you probably won't understand this and I certainly understand we are going to cause you problems but we need to pull the SDA referral paperwork for Julia. She has something going on and it just isn't getting any better."

Vitaly's response surprised me, "Michael, I understand, I too can tell she is very unhappy and do not believe what the psychologist told us."

Vitaly called Konstantin, left a message and in 10 minutes an irate Konstantin called me back, saying, "I have already submitted the documents to the SDA!" This was after he had told us the day before that we were too late to submit them because it was the weekend and they would not be looked at until Monday at the earliest.

"Konstantin, you said you still needed some information before you submitted the papers, how is it now that you say they already have them?" I said.

"Michael, you just don't understand how this works," he preached trying to cover his tracks. "You don't know what problems you have caused me. What will the SDA think of me?"

All I could think at this moment was, *'if Konstantin had been there for the second SDA meeting and not left us with George, who was a nice man but had not worked in the system for over a year, we probably would not be having this conversation. Konstantin was off working with other couples, juggling people and collecting fees. He took his eye off the ball was blaming all of the problems on Paula and me.'*

"Konstantin, there shouldn't be a problem here. The SDA gave us referrals for two children that didn't want to be adopted. Surely they'll understand that it wasn't our fault and give us a third meeting. We've met two other children, Nadya and Albina, who really touched us and they *want* to be adopted. We would like to try to adopt *both* of them. They've started to become attached to us. Maybe we should move forward with these girls? What do you think?"

After a few calls back and forth, Konstantin told me, "I have pulled the referral for Julia M and will file a petition for a third meeting based upon these facts."

Little did we know…

**BLOG Entry** - Hi everybody,

What an emotional roller coaster! If you have been following this blog, you no doubt read a few days ago that Julia was doing great. Well, we spent the weekend with her and in a nutshell she would not talk to us or even try. Our translator spent an hour talking to her and got nowhere.

Last night, we made a very hard decision; to pull the petition to adopt Julia from the court. We do not know what this will mean other than we may very well be coming home after a month with just our suitcase, and no daughter. Our hope is that we might have a chance to adopt one of the many other girls at the orphanage that were very excited to be with us and REALLY wanted to join our family ... I expect by the end of the day today, we will have

```
some clarity and hear from our facilitator
regarding any options that we may have.

Please pray for Julia:)
```

Vitaly spent the entire next day preparing a new petition for a third referral meeting and then put it on the train to be delivered to Kiev the next morning.

*TRAVEL NOTE: In Ukraine, passenger trains have many conductors that take care of the passengers traveling in their cars and for a few greevna [$5 U.S.] They are glad to carry documents and small packages from place to place for you. It's like a cheap version of UPS.*

The next morning Konstantin called and said, "Okay, I have filed the new petition and you must now wait for the third meeting. I want you and Paula to go to the orphanage everyday and spend time with these new girls you want to adopt and get very close to them. Then when we meet with the SDA we can show them how much they want to be adopted by you. They will see this as a good thing and your chances will be good."

At this point, Paula and I didn't think things were working out too badly other than the issues with Konstantin and the way he handled the SDA appointments, so we did as we were told.

Vitaly decided this would be a good time to go home and see his wife and baby daughter in Nikolayev so he left to buy a ticket for the 10-hour bus ride home. When he returned, he gave us Sasha's phone number and told us, "You will be okay here without me.  Call me if you have any troubles."  And he was gone.

*September 23rd*
*Melitopol, Ukraine*

Paula and I were celebrating our 15th wedding anniversary in Ukraine together, and I didn't want it to casually pass even if we were in the middle of nowhere.

"Honey, what would you like to do today for our anniversary?" I asked.

"Well, we can go to Classic," she replied.

"But we do that every night.  Let's do something special."

"Hmmm, that is special.  Guess what?  There isn't anything else to do here."

You see, my wife is very practical and as much as I wanted to do something special for our anniversary, just being here was special but let's face it, Melitopol is not San Francisco, the Caribbean, New York or Chicago … there are no theaters, dancing, museums or nightlife.

"It's Ukraine."

We decided to take the walk to Classic restaurant so we bundled up for the quickly dropping temperature.  Thirty minutes later, we arrived at Classic only to find that there was a wedding in progress and they were closed to the public. So being resourceful — off to the market we went. Buying our usual yogurt, cheese, olive oil and some fruit, we headed back to the hotel where we spent the evening together eating, and toasting our anniversary with some vodka while we watched the movie "300" on the computer. I was happy just to be with Paula. That was special enough for me.

# Nadya and Albina

*September 24th*
*Melitopol, Ukraine*

This morning, Paula woke early and said, "Let's get the kids a ping-pong table."

I replied, "Why would you want to do that?" thinking that it would be impossible to find one in Melitopol and Paula must not have slept through the night.

"I am sure we can find one and it's the perfect thing for the kids to do when they are stuck inside."

"You will never find one here." I said as we left for a morning walk.

We went to the open market and strolled around in awe of the deals and wished we had this type of market in Cleveland. I mean, where can you buy a great looking insulated leather jacket for $35? As my son, Tyler, would say, "It's crazy."

Paula tried on about a hundred pairs of shoes and I kept my eyes open for things we might bring home for Grace.

On the way back to the hotel, we stopped at the grocery to pick up some water and passed a toy store. We decided to take a quick look to see if there were some games or something we could take the orphanage.  We weren't there five minutes when I heard Paula behind me, "Hey Mike, here's a ping-pong table!"  There it was, in all its glory.

"They'll probably lose all the balls in a week," I said, still not getting the point.  Paula stood her ground and we arranged through Vitaly (with Valery's blessing) to have the table delivered to the orphanage later that same day.

Like so many other times, my wife has an intuition about things that I sometimes just don't understand and have learned to go with, although it's still hard to keep my mouth shut.

Around noon, we headed to the internot, as we did every day, to see the children and await delivery of the ping-pong table.

Happy to see me, Valery said, "Michael, you and I will play the first game."

The ping-pong table arrived as promised and the guys that delivered it were very nice, following Valery's assistant from building to building until she found the perfect place for the table, which happened to be right outside the director's office.  I was inside talking to him and Paula entered to hand him a large plastic urn containing about 500 ping-pong balls explaining through Vitaly that he should, "Hand them out and have the children return the balls to you after they play.  That way they may last for a couple of months."

Valery took the balls from Paula and offered her a drink, which she politely declined.

A little later, the sun was going down and it was time for me to play ping-pong with Valery. Before we pick up our paddles he convinced me that we should have a couple of shots of his favorite cognac to which I obliged, solely on a political basis. Even though I felt close to Valery, my experience in Ukraine has awakened, or at least heightened ,my sense of awareness of the simple fact that we aren't in control and anything can happen — so we always need to defer to our host's requests. That was my reasoning anyway, and it sounded good at the time.

Politics aside, Valery proved to be a worthy opponent. I played a lot of ping-pong when I was a younger but I never knew that ping-pong was a national pastime in Ukraine. Valery, at 68, was still my better even though he probably had not played in many years. The gallery of children watching us were cheering him on and he didn't disappoint. After every point on the younger American, he raised his arms in victory and laughed loudly. I was enjoying losing to Valery more than if I was winning, which I never did experience during our extended play.

After Valery had beaten me more than 15 times and his ego was filled, he moved aside and allowed the children to play. They turned out to be more my speed as I knocked them off one by one. The mood was festive as they danced around the table trying to make me lose my focus, but it wasn't going to happen.

Play went on well into the night, and at the end I was victorious, and undefeated. Not because I was so good but because I was lucky and just one stroke faster.

*September 26th*
*Melitopol, Ukraine*

Still reeling from our experience with Julia and not knowing if what we were doing made any sense, we went to the orphanage everyday to play with the children and get to know Albina and Nadya.

We didn't know what would happen at the third SDA meeting and were concerned that if we got too close to the girls and things didn't work out, that they would be crushed. On the other hand, if we didn't spend a lot of time with them, we wouldn't have a chance with the SDA, according to Konstantin.

Then there was the question of one or two girls. As older parents, it seemed a little crazy but we thought two would be the right number in light of the fact that the girls would always have each other, learning would be easier, and we would have a truly international family and so on and so on. This rational seemed to make sense at the moment, so we moved forward.

Both Nadya and Albina are nice 11-year-old girls with very different personalities and agendas. Time after time, from the director to the teachers, we were told that we needed to be careful with Albina because she was a leader and always got her way, by hook or by crook.

They said, "Be careful. She is manipulative and very smart."

Paula joked and said, "Then she will get along very well as an American girl." Nadya always seemed happy. She was a performer and singer, but shy in a funny kind of way.

I know it is not much to go on, but Paula and I both felt that these girls would fit well into our family, so we headed right down the path with them, knowing that we would be happy with either one or both of the girls.

*September 27th*
*Melitopol, Ukraine*

Paula woke up and said, "Let's take Nadya and Albina on a picnic."

We didn't know where we would take them because the area surrounding the orphanage is generally farmland, but figured that we could find somewhere nice. So, off we went to the market to pick up a few things they might like to eat. Our list of food included cheese, bread, sardines, a couple of pizzas from our favorite spot, dessert and drinks. Nothing unusual but we bought enough food to feed a small army.

Upon arriving, the girls and their entourage met our car with smiles and followed us, as always, from building to building, as we walked around the internot. We briefly met up with Valery who, after a series of bear hugs agreed that a picnic would be fine. Nika was up for a picnic even though she didn't know what a picnic was, and asked us if her two girlfriends could join us.

We said, "Sure, bring them along." But then they disappeared.

A few minutes later, they returned with a single piece of bread (their lunch) they had bought from a street vendor.

We crossed the street, cutting through a few neighbors' yards, and down a narrow path past a snow-white goat who sat and stared at us like we were from another planet — which in the eyes of the locals, we were.

**One of the neighbors**

Walking into the modest-size forest, we followed the girls, who seemed to know exactly where they wanted to take us. Thirty minutes later the woods opened up to a field and all of the sudden, I realized they were lost. The special place Albina and Nika were taking us had eluded them, but the exact place no longer mattered. What mattered now was the food. Everybody was hungry and the task at hand was to find a place to eat — and fast!

We decided that anyplace would be fine so we stopped, sat down, spread out our feast and Paula started serving. Again, there was little conversation as there was not much to say. Eyes opened wide as Paula unloaded our market bag. The girls never get to eat like this at the internot.

For the next five minutes, Paula and I sat back and watched in amazement as Albina, Nadya, Nika and her two friends ate everything. I have yet to experience anything quite like it. Every last bit of food was gone except for a few slices of bread, which the girls asked, "Can we take this home?" We had enough food for 15 people and it was gone in a flash. It was the fastest picnic in history.

**Paula, Julia, Nadya, Nika and her friends**

As soon as we were done eating, the girls all ran off to find a natural toilet and Paula and I lost track of them for a few minutes. It was a bit unnerving, but this was their territory and we were the visitors so we just waited and talked about the rest of our day.

**Nadya, Paula and Albina**

Out of the corner of my eye I saw a movement in the woods and alerted Paula. We hid behind a tree and watched closely to see what it was. My fear was that it might be a pack of dogs, as they run freely in Ukraine, and can be very dangerous. There were many stories of people who had disappeared and were never found again — falling victim to the wild dogs.

I was reluctant to call out to the girls because that would only draw attention to us and we didn't know what we were dealing with. Being so far out in the woods and away from assistance, we sat quietly and continued to survey the surroundings.

There it was again, a shadow moving behind the trees some 100 yards away. I couldn't make out a defined shape but it was definitely bigger than a dog and there were several of them.

I thought I better get closer, but Paula grabbed my arm, "Where do you think you're going? You can't leave me here and what are you going to do if they come after you?"

"Well, we can't just stand here," I said. "What about the girls?"

Then the shadows moved past again in the distant tree line and we saw they were human. "What could they want?" Paula said. "Why are they all the way out here?" I was getting a very uncomfortable feeling like being in the middle of that old movie *Deliverance*. Then, POW — POW — POW, guns rang out. The girls reappeared, ran to our side and we all looked into the woods together. They were hunters in camouflage and had found their prey. Thankfully it wasn't us! They didn't even know we were here. Nevertheless, we all went running in the opposite direction back towards the internot.

It was a most unusual picnic. But, after all…

"It's Ukraine."

*September 28th*
*Melitopol, Ukraine*

We had been coming to the orphanage now for several days when we decided it was a good time to talk to the girls individually. We needed to dig a little deeper into their background and feelings, so we took each of them with our new friend, Nika (who volunteered to translate), for a walk in the village and told them about our family, our house, Grace, Cleveland, etc. We asked them why they wanted to be adopted, and about their families.

We asked each one…

"Is there anything you would like to ask us?"

Nadya replied, "No, I just want a Mama," and hugged Paula.

Albina, on the other hand, asked some very pointed questions. "Will I have my own room?"

I said, "We probably could arrange that."

She then added, "Will I have my own computer?" and then "Cell phone?"

I said to Paula "Oh man, what have we got here?"

It was not until later when Paula and I were talking that she said, "It's hard to know where that came from, Albina has been in an orphanage for seven years so she couldn't possibly even know what she is asking for. She must have just seen this stuff on TV."

Both girls wanted desperately to have a family and get out of this place — not so much because they hated the orphanage but because they felt alone in their respective little worlds and worried about their life and their future.

*September 30th*
*Melitopal, Ukraine*

A funny thing happened while we were strolling around the orphanage grounds... there were about 15 kids walking with us, as usual, performing their various talents and Albina touched me on the shoulder to watch her. She then did one of those backbend things where they extend backward and then walkover. I laughed loudly and clapped and then the show began. Every child lined up to show us what kind of gymnastic talent they had beginning with front flips and progressing to jumping up in the air and landing in a split. Every time one child would do a trick, the other kids would try to outdo them.

All I kept thinking was "ouch, I bet that hurt," but they kept going and going like the little Energizer Bunny. After 30 minutes, the tricks were getting progressively more dangerous, so I called a halt before anyone got hurt.

*October 1st*
*Melitopol, Ukraine*

After an early morning walk through the park across the street from our hotel, Paula and I spent time on Skype talking to Grace and June about school and the fact that nothing important was going on. We were in a bit of limbo, ready to come home and missed Grace terribly.

Around noon, we took our daily trek to the internot, walked with the kids and attended a village soccer match in an adjoining field. Soccer was one of the few pastimes that didn't cost money in this faraway village so most of the able-bodied men were quite engaged and quite skilled. It was much like watching a pro match because these guys played like a team in a major league. There was one young man in particular that I thought ran faster than any human I'd ever seen and scored an unassisted goal from almost 40 yards out!

**Local soccer between the internot and Graveyard**

The village residents lined the field cheering not their team, but individuals, as the game was being played by teams made up of village players. It was kind of like when you were a child and the two biggest kids selected from all the kids in the neighborhood until no one was left.

The girls sat with us so proudly and Nika translated as the locals looked on at the curious Americans. It was a high point on our trip to Melitopol.

# Disbelief

*October 3rd*
*Melitopol, Ukraine*

We're pretty confident that we will be getting another referral in the next day or so because of all of the mistakes the SDA has made along the way, so to kill some time while until we hear from Konstantin, we sat in our hotel room — me, reading a great Orson Scott Card book and Paula, catching up on our blog for the past few days — she is such a great writer.

```
Paula's Blog Entry:
It is pitch black by now at the orphanage
... there is no outdoor lighting, but it
is safe ... the kids run from the dining
hall to the main dormitory building and
one of the teachers, Marina, is playing
disco music for the kids ...

The girls all run and change into
something lightweight and start dancing.
Funny thing is, Mike and I hate the music
in this country ... it is all the same
with the same 1980s disco beat ... they
play it everywhere ... in the cabs, in the
```

restaurants, in the hotel ... you cannot get away from it ... it's like robot music, but tonight, we forget about that and dance with the kids like this is the best music we've ever heard.

I've never seen Mike dance and I've been married to him for 15 years, but tonight, he's dancing, and the kids think we're cool ... After a little warm-up on the floor, the boys started with the handstands, flips, and head spins, and I started to get nervous ... the cognac was wearing off for Michael and there was no way he was going to be doing any of that.

At 9 p.m., Sasha, our driver, shows up to rescue us and thank goodness his vehicle is still running even though the red warning light keeps flashing on his dashboard. We say good night to the kids and off we go for a luxurious evening in our Seven Star Hotel (that means it has a toilet, but you have to supply your own paper).

Paula had just finished this entry and we were feeling very positive about how things would turn out when the phone rang.

It's Konstantin who says flatly, "The SDA has turned down your request for a third meeting."

We were in shock ... plain and simple. We never even considered that the SDA wouldn't grant us another meeting. We were even thinking that they might cut some of the red tape for us after everything we had been through. Guess again.

"It's Ukraine."

A couple of weeks prior, we'd had a family friend who was connected to a high-level Kiev city councilman get in touch with the director of the SDA to put in a good word us because we didn't want to take any chances. We figured that it was "in the bag" and we were in good shape until he notified us that his call fell on deaf ears because the SDA is a federal government agency and they would do him no favors.

He also said, "I am very sorry for you because the entire Ukraine adoption system is constructed in a way to take money from people like you and I am ashamed." All the way down the line from the payoffs to the delays, anything that will bring money into the local economies is fair game.

So there it is folks — straight from a government official, just in case you have been wondering.

After Konstantin's call, we decided to go directly to Kiev and speak to the SDA deputy director who takes meetings Wednesdays from 3 to 5 p.m. to address problems like ours. We asked Vitaly to join us and he agreed, but Konstantin who had written us off at this point said, "I will go if you insist but it is not good for my reputation and there is nothing I can do to help you now."

I don't blame him because he had already collected every penny he could from us, and also knew something he never bothered to share — *the SDA NEVER ever gives a third referral*. He had convinced us otherwise and left Albina and Nadya to suffer in the wake.

Everything was totally out of our control and falling apart around us. We needed to get to Kiev as soon as possible and convince the SDA that these mistakes were not our fault and we had found these two wonderful children who we had become very close to and who wanted to come home with us. It would be good for everybody and a very easy adoption to complete.

Sasha drove us out to the internot and we took the girls into a small room where we made a video of them making a personal plea to the SDA to allow us to adopt them. They said that they loved us and that they loved each other and wanted so much to go to America and become part of our family.

We thought we could use this video as part of our SDA meeting to show how much we had invested in the children. We left shortly after this visit and told the girls that we were going to Kiev where we thought we could convince the SDA to allow us to adopt them, but that we could not promise anything. They were sad but hugged us and wished us, "Good luck with those people. When will you come back to get us?" They really didn't understand what was happening but we couldn't explain it either.  As we left them I knew that I would never forget the look of longing and sadness on their faces.

The next evening, Sasha took us to the rail station and helped us buy our tickets.  He also refused to let us pay him for this trip.  He patiently waited with us for almost an hour to make sure we got on the train okay and even offered to get me a cup of coffee as a gift.  He was such a kind man.  Another overnight on the train and we arrived in Kiev at about 7 a.m.

*October 5th*
*Kiev, Ukraine*

Vitaly was waiting for us after his all-night bus ride from Nikolayev.  We spent most of the day strategizing our meeting and felt very prepared with our notes and video of the girls.  Our reasoning seemed sound because we thought that the SDA just didn't understand that there had been problems outside of our control, and that we had developed new relationships with a couple of children who did, in fact, want to be adopted.  These girls were ready to go, and we were willing to jump through all of the necessary hoops to make that happen.  All the SDA had to do was understand the mishaps and allow us to wrap-up our business.

We were exhausted emotionally, physically and every other way you could think of, and at 2:30 pm we started the long walk to the SDA office — wanting to make sure we were there in plenty of time to present our case. When 3 o'clock rolled around, we walked into the SDA building and were invited upstairs. We were introduced to the deputy director, a pleasant looking woman with blond hair and an air of confidence.

Vitaly, Paula and I sat down and were prepared to present our case when she said, "It is the law in Ukraine that you can only have two referrals. A referral is the document you received from our office that allows you to visit a child. You have had two referrals and I am sorry but you are done — you can go home to America now."

Paula, Vitaly and I looked at each other in disbelief. That was it? Everything Konstantin told us had been a lie. What about the children he told us to get close to — to visit everyday? What about Nadya and Albina?

We were numb. Have you ever had that feeling, when you simply have nothing to say, nowhere to go, nothing you can do — when you are completely, utterly powerless?

We walked out of the deputy director's office without saying a word to the director or to each other. We were all trying to make sense of what had just happened and dealing with our disbelief that it was over. We walked and walked with Vitaly who was probably just as depressed as we were but he never said so. He had done his best to make it happen for the girls, and us, but in his own eyes he had failed. In our eyes, he was a champion who had just been dethroned and beaten by his own people.

An hour later, we arrived back at our hotel. I emailed a simple message to our travel agent, Cindy. "Cindy, it's over. Get us out of here tomorrow, please!" and I hit the send button. I was feeling so bad for Paula who was convinced that the government would see the errors in their system and make things right.

# Frontier to the Rescue

*October 15th*
*Chagrin Falls, Ohio*

Paula and I returned from Ukraine a week or so ago exhausted and happy to be home but still in shock over the events of the preceding seven weeks. Grace was there to greet us when we arrived, as was June, and it was only a couple of days before we started settling back into the Cleveland way of life.

As usual we would be up at 6:30 a.m. to cook breakfast and prepare a school lunch for Grace (a lunch that most mothers would envy.) Paula is a wonderful cook, and having such an interest in health and nutrition, Grace often has a breakfast of fresh blueberries with homemade cashew butter, followed by kasha with Amish raw butter and agave sweetener. Lunch is equally gourmet.

We didn't talk too much about the trip or the outcome for a few days because it was too painful and after four years of trying to adopt, we just needed a break. I just couldn't help but thinking about what the SDA deputy director had said when we were told to go home.

Even though the Ukraine government doesn't acknowledge it, you can petition to adopt specific children based upon the relationship formed during a hosting trip. In the words of the SDA deputy director "If you wish to adopt these two girls, you will need to start over and submit all new paperwork. Then you should host them. We will know then that you have a legal relationship with these children."

Remember how I said that it was over? Well, there is also another old saying, "It's not over 'til it's over" and "Never, never, never, give up."

So, I sat down at my computer and *Googled*, "Ukraine Hosting." It was mid-November and I thought that maybe, just maybe, I could find a hosting company that would go the extra mile and help Paula and I host Albina and Nadya for the upcoming holidays.

I searched and searched, made call after call and left message after message. When I was just about ready to give in to the reality that we were, in fact, done, an angel named Maggie answered my call and our prayers. The company was Frontier Horizon, and Maggie and I spoke at length about our journey and predicament. She just happened to be walking through Dulles airport in D.C., on her way to Ukraine!

Things were looking up when she told me, "Yes, we are conducting a hosting for the holidays. Why don't you send me the specifics and I will see what we can do."

I hung up the phone with renewed hope and couldn't wait to tell Paula.

An hour later, I sent Maggie photos of the girls, contacted Vitaly and started the ball rolling again with no regard for where the ball might take us.

Frontier Horizon is a great organization that facilitates hosting programs mostly from Ukraine. Like many nonprofit organizations of this type, they have relationships with orphanage directors and host children starting from about six years old, to families in the U.S. They conduct several programs for summer and holidays. For children, most of whom have never been out of the orphanage — much less to the USA, this is their first step towards adoption.

Frontier Horizon is not an adoption agency but does have good relationships with people who can act on your behalf to facilitate the in-country adoption process.

Once Maggie had the information about the orphanage and the girls, she checked with Vincent Rosini, Director of Frontier, who has spent a good part of his life helping children find homes. He called and said, "Michael, I think we can make this happen if the director agrees." Great news for us, especially on such short notice!

Now it gets complicated… again.

Maggie introduced me to Dima, a facilitator who works with some of their host families, and we laid out a plan. We would need to get Valery to agree to the hosting since our orphanage in Melitopol had never hosted their children before, get visas and passports for the girls, and then get everything approved by the U.S. Embassy in Kiev. The cost to us would be about $7,000 [U.S.] for both girls. Everything seemed reasonable and if Vitaly helped us, we thought that we could make it before the cutoff date for hosting of November 14th. You see, we planned for the children to travel to the U.S. on December 19th and it was already November 4th, so time was short.

The next day, Dima contacted Vitaly and asked if he would introduce him to the director, Valery. Vitaly was happy to do so but Valery had never hosted children from his orphanage in the 50 years that he'd run the place. He trusted Vitaly but not this new guy, Dima. This was not big a problem and Vitaly called him a few times to reassure him that everything was on the up and up. He agreed to go to Zaporizhzhya to get the passports for the girls.

He told us, "The man that runs the passport office is a good friend of mine and owes me a favor so he will do it for me fast." The passports needed to be applied for and then sent to Kiev for approval, and then back via rail, because there are no express mail companies like Federal Express in Melitopol.

Paula and I were getting excited to have the girls come over the holidays and started making our plans while Valery took care of the legal part for us.

A week later, nothing had happened. We were starting to get nervous so Vitaly called Valery to ask him what was going on. "It is not a problem. You will get the passports soon," he said.

It was starting to feel like "It's Ukraine" all over again.

Valery was going to pay the man at the passport office to make it move faster but still nothing… nothing… nothing. Dima was patient but concerned, because the papers we needed (medical, etc.) were not coming either.

"What can we do?" Paula asked me. "If we miss this deadline and miss the hosting, then everything we have been trying to accomplish over the past year will be in vain. Albina and Nadya will be stuck there."

It was upsetting to say the least, but our hands were tied. As a last resort, Vitaly took an overnight train to see Valery and get to the bottom of the issue.

Walking into the orphanage, Vitaly asked a confused Valery, "What is taking so long? Why have you not done as you promised?"

Valery said, "What do you mean? I always do what I say I will do, and you will have your papers soon, just as I promised."

"That was two weeks ago and Paula and Michael will not have the girls now because we do not have the papers!" Vitaly said.

Valery replied, "You mean you need them right now?"

"Of course!"

"I didn't know you needed them by a specific date. I will go to Zaporizhzhya tomorrow and force my friend to expedite them."

Vitaly smiled and left after offering to make the trip himself to make sure the job got done.

Four days later, December 11th, we got a call from Dima. "I got all of the papers from Valery and I can go to the Embassy to get the girls a visa. Albina and Nadya are coming to America next week!"

# The Eight-Day Dossier

As part of our grand scheme, Paula, Dima and I were formulating a plan to adopt Albina and Nadya and hoping to at least get one of the girls. The idea was that if we could get the hosting together in time for Christmas, we could also work concurrently on a new dossier and submit it with a special petition for the girls based upon our hosting them. Our hope was that we would be approved quickly as a result of the hosting and return in the spring or early summer to bring the girls home.

Paula had put together somewhere in the neighborhood of eight dossiers over the past four years so we were not worried about the process other than the sheer amount of time and effort that would be required of her.

Then came a call from Dima on November 12th. "Paula, there is an opportunity for you and Michael, but I don't know if it is too late. They have extended the date for accepting dossiers until November 22nd. If I can submit yours, then it is possible to come back to Ukraine soon after the New Year. What are the expiration dates of your current dossier?"

In Ukraine, your dossier is only good for a period of six months after it is officially apostilled.

"Well, I think everything is still good except for the Home Study and one other document so we should be able to get that updated and back to you very soon," Paula said.

"That is very good news. Maybe things are changing and it is good fortune for you," Dima replied.

We hung up the phone ...

It was not even an hour before Paula slowly walked into the kitchen with her head hanging low and said, "The whole dossier has expired."

"What do you mean, it's expired?" I said.

Her words came slowly, "I just looked at all of the papers and I thought we had a month or more but some have already expired and the rest expire next week. It's impossible to get this together in time."

"Okay honey, let's just see what is possible. I am going to take off next week from work and we can work full-time on this together." And so it started. I call it the eight-day dossier.

We had the help of many public servants who went out of their way to help us make this happen in record time. There were a few things that we organized that will apply to any dossier and may help others.

*NOTE: Most, if not all, documents need to be notarized, certified and apostilled. Try to get all documents notarized by the same person. Then you can get them certified (this is to certify that the notary is registered) in one local county office. Lastly, collect all of your papers and make only one trip to the state capital to get them apostilled.*

The "Home Study" needed to be updated to our current conditions and changed to allow for two children. We contacted the person who originally conducted our home study (which took six weeks), "We need this changed and we must have it back in two days."

"Impossible," she said.

"Well, I'll bring it to you and pick it up. It's a small change and I will still pay you the full update fee if you can pull it off," I said. [Keep in mind that the economy was not doing so well in the fall of 2008 and home studies were probably not a good business to be in.]

"The fee will be $700 and I will make the required changes as long as there has been no material change in your circumstances," she responded. We received the updated home study two days later.

Fingerprints: Off to the local police station for a local check… three hours and done!

FBI background check: With the help of the local office they were back in 7 business days.

The I-600 and all other documents were completed in record time.

It was 4:45 p.m. and I was in Columbus, Ohio at the Department of State where they had just handed me a stack of about 30 documents that had all been apostilled. With lots of help, lots of negotiating and with the Grace of God, we had all our paperwork back in hand in eight business days. I headed to FedEx and for $221 sent the package to Dima who was anxiously waiting to submit it to the SDA before the year-end deadline. The fastest FedEx delivery you can get to Kiev is about five to seven days. If the documents arrived in five days, we would be fine, but seven would miss the deadline.

We'd performed miracles. Now all we could do was wait.

Five days later, we get a frantic Skype call from Dima -

"Michael, I just received the package and everything looks good but the Power of Attorney is done wrong. It needs to be *open* so I can assign a regional facilitator like Vitaly to use it. Please redo the document, have it apostilled, and send it right away."

"Okay, I will," I said. "But now we have missed the SDA deadline right?"

"No, I will take this package and submit it right now. They probably won't even notice the mistake on the Power of Attorney, but you need to get me a correct one as soon as possible, just in case," Dima said and hung up.

It seemed like the fun would never end. It was like being stuck in some kind of comical Steve Martin or Chevy Chase movie where secret cameras are strategically positioned to watch what you will do when faced with the impossible.

There was only one thing I could do at this point — get a new POA and send it to Kiev ASAP. I took care of the revision the next day and then made the trip downtown to get the document certified. Of course, it still needed to be apostilled so after leaving the downtown Cleveland office, I made the two-hour drive to Columbus again. I had called ahead to make sure there would be someone available to apostille the papers and a wonderful woman, Mary, who sympathized with our situation was there waiting for me when I arrived.

The apostilling was a one-minute process and after paying $3.00, I was once again rushing to get to FedEx. $221 later, the new documents were on their way to Dima and I was on my way home.

# Third Trip to Ukraine

*December 1st*
*Chagrin Falls, Ohio*

I arrive at my Starbucks office every morning about 7:30 a.m., grab a cup of coffee and login to talk to my programmers who are located in different parts of the world (mostly Russia). This morning was no different, other than the email I received from Dima that started, "Michael, I have good news. Your dossier was received and approved. Your appointment is next week in Kiev, December 8th at 3 p.m."

A flood of emotions came over me including surprise, happiness, fear and anxiety — we are not ready!

This email required that I call Paula right away. "Honey, you are not going to believe this but we just got our invitation to go back to Ukraine and we leave in less than a week!"

"There is no way we can do that. The girls are coming for the holidays and we don't have anybody to stay with Grace. This is the train wreck!" she says.

"No," I said with a smile, "It's Ukraine."

I emailed Dima, "Dima, is it possible to move the appointment until after the hosting so we can tell them that we have hosted the girls and that is how we met them? I am afraid that if we don't, the SDA will think we met the girls illegally and won't give us the referral."

Dima replied in just a few minutes, "Michael, it is your choice, but if you move the appointment, you cannot even go to Ukraine until next November, a year from now."

"Okay, somehow, we will be there." I wrote and then drove directly home.

I took the rest of the day off and spent the next few hours with Paula trying to figure out how we could make this all work. Our ultimate decision was that we would go to Ukraine, meet Vitaly in Melitopol, (if) we received the referrals and conduct as much of the adoption paperwork as possible prior to the girls visiting us for the Christmas holiday. This was all well and good but if we didn't get the referrals it wouldn't make for such a great holiday because the girls would come to visit us knowing we could not adopt them.

We also still had to deal with my work and who would take care of Grace while we were gone. We couldn't ask June again because we had already taken her away from her home for seven weeks, but we called her just to confirm our feelings only to be surprised again — in a never-ending string of surprises.

"Paula," June said, "I started this with you and Michael and I am going to finish it. Get me a ticket and I'll be there." Maybe some of you are lucky enough to have a 'June' in your life.

As I mentioned before, I am blessed to be able to conduct my business remotely but this was bordering on the ridiculous. I had already been away for almost six weeks and even though I have a great team working with me, the time difference and lack of Internet access make it a challenge. So I was to spend the next week planning and arranging my work schedule to continue in my absence. Oh yes, all while we were getting everything else ready for our trip.

*December 5th*
*Chagrin Falls, Ohio*

June arrived from Florida and I picked her up in Akron, Ohio. She was her ever-positive self and just shook her head when I told her our latest story. June raised six children and then took me in when I was 15-years old. We always had other stray kids that lived with us from time to time and June sometimes reminded me of the nursery rhyme, "the old woman who lived in a shoe."

When June's kids went off to live their respective lives, she even helped raise one of her daughter's two young girls. It seems this was the role God planned for her, to care for his children. This is June Farris, a kind and loving woman full of wonder, and unending compassion.

**Grace and June**

When June was settled and comfortable in her room upstairs, we went over all the meal planning, school activities, bills and other household issues that she might encounter while we were away. She took all of our "lists" in stride and told us, "Don't worry about a thing. Grace and I will be just fine." The same thing she always says. "Do you know how long you will be gone on this trip?"

"We should be back December 19th with the girls for the holiday hosting," I said. "Then if everything works out, we will go back after the holidays — maybe in February or March to finalize the adoption."

*December 7th*
*Chagrin Falls, Ohio*

After some quick negotiating with our travel agent, Cindy, we were able to pull a flight together. So again, we said 'goodbye' to Grace and June and headed back to Ukraine to try once again.

---

### <u>Our new plan</u>

I thought it might be interesting to tell you our plan prior to this trip so you can see for yourself just how dramatically things can change in the adoption process.

The plan this time is that we will attend our meeting at the SDA with Dima, get the referrals for Albina and Nadya because we filed a petition for them and head off to Melitopol the following day. As I have said many times before, this is our plan, but will most likely not happen this way.

With our referrals in hand, we will the travel to Melitopol where we will meet up with Vitaly, start the paperwork for the girls and do our best to overcome a few big hurdles that we are still facing. If we can get all the approvals from siblings, then we can submit the final paperwork back to the SDA in Kiev and they will process it while we are hosting the girls back in Cleveland for the holidays.

One of the biggest challenges will be to get Nadya's grandmother and brother who don't want her to be adopted to agree to her adoption.

Nadya told us when we met that nobody had been to see her in years, but as it turns out she has a grandmother and brother that visit her regularly. Valery even went to visit the grandmother a month ago to convince her that adoption was the best thing for Nadya, but she wouldn't even talk to him. Our new friend Maggie told me that in many cases once the grandmother meets us and understands that Nadya will have a much better life, she will probably change her mind, but we'll have to see how it goes.

I wrote this passage while sitting on an Aerosvit flight from JFK, though Paula and I were not happy when we boarded this plane. We felt like it was God was telling us, "I'm sending you back to Ukraine. Don't expect too much. And by the way, you won't be sleeping tonight." The plane was old and cramped with poor service, worn-out seats and the movie they were showing was on a 10-inch screen in the front of the cabin. We aren't complaining — as a matter of fact, it was just kind of funny. We arrived in Kiev 45 minutes later, met our driver and rode to our apartment to get an hour or two of sleep before the adventure continued.

*December 8th*
*Kiev, Ukraine*

Kiev is cold and the flat grey sky that blankets the city looks just like home in Cleveland. Winter here can be brutal and this looks like the start of a long one. The potholes here make the ones in New York City seem insignificant. We knew we were back in Kiev, where the government is under-funded and can't afford to keep up their streets.

Our apartment this time, was close to the U.S. Embassy, on the 12th floor and actually the nicest we've stayed in to date with two bedrooms, a living room, separate kitchen and Internet for about $110 a night. Not bad for Kiev. The only problem — there is nowhere to eat nearby and morning coffee is not to be found — a challenge, but in the grand scheme of things, a very small one.

Paula and I crashed on the couch for a couple of hours and then walked about a mile to the SDA office. It was a nice day to walk and when we arrived, we met Dima, a tall, good looking young man that would be facilitating this adoption attempt.

**Dima and Paula**

This was our fourth visit to the SDA and I was still uncomfortable, but at least we knew this time that we didn't need to bring a suit and dress up for our interview. I wore Khaki pants and a blue pullover and Paula wore black slacks and a pretty sweater. (In case you were interested — I was.)

We were most anxious about the reaction we would receive when we presented the petition for the girls and were very relieved when the door opened and the SDA psychologists saw Dima. They were obviously fond of him, smiling and making small talk. In that one moment, everything changed and we were "okay." They offered us a seat and started to look over the paperwork.

"Well, everything seems to be in order," one of them says and Paula's eyes dart in my direction in disbelief. I was thinking that this couldn't be happening — they're actually being nice!

"You can go visit both girls but you realize that they have siblings that are in orphanages and you will need to adopt them, too," she says firmly but with a very friendly tone.

We knew this might happen. It was part of our plan and weren't shocked although the road ahead just became a little longer. We would now need to meet all of the siblings and ask them to write letters saying that they didn't want to be adopted, but that we were welcome to adopt their sisters. In Ukraine, if you adopt a child that has siblings in an orphanage, it is the law that you must adopt them too, unless they refuse to be adopted.

Over the next 30 minutes, they worked on the referrals for all four children and we walked out happy, but knowing we would be facing an uphill battle.

After leaving the SDA building and a couple of high-fives, we headed up the street to the same little Internet café to have our dossier copied, but this time it was also different. When we walked through the door the woman at the reception desk saw Dima and asked, "Well, what can I do for *you*?"

Dima handed her the large dossier. "I need this copied, please."

"This isn't a problem. I will do it for you right now."

Paula just looked at me and smiled.

One hour later we're off to purchase our train tickets to Melitopol and then back to our new apartment. It had been a good day for us and we recognized that we were being watched over and were thankful. The next evening we head back to Melitopol.

# The Siblings

*December 10th*
*Melitopol, Ukraine*

We boarded the train at 7:40 p.m. for the now all too familiar trip to Melitopol, but this time we had learned to pack blankets around the heating pipes under the bed so it was more comfortable and we actually did get some sleep.

I forgot to tell the conductor to wake us for the Melitopol stop but did set my alarm clock for what I thought would be an hour before we detrained. When the alarm went off, the train was stopping and we opened our eyes to find it was already at the Melitopol station.

"Oh poop! We are going to miss our stop," I said and we moved as fast as we could to jam our belongings back into our suitcases and drag them down the narrow hallway just in time — I mean seconds — before the train blew the whistle and rolled forward on to the next destination.

Hearts pounding, half asleep and hungry, we greeted Vitaly and Sasha with wimpy smiles.

"If we missed that stop, we might have been lost for weeks," Paula said, trying to make light of our mishap.

The Seven Stars hotel never looked so good to me as when we arrived. It was even colder here than in Kiev with the thermometer hovering somewhere around 30 degrees and the clouds rolling in for winter. Victoria, the all-night hotel monitor, who slept on the couch in the lobby jumped up to let us in when Vitaly knocked on the window and took us straight to our room. She made me a quick cup of coffee and then went back to sleep.

Paula, Vitaly and I sat in the room for an hour putting our plan together for the upcoming week. We were hoping to get all of the letters from the siblings and grandmother and the rest of the paperwork together before we left for the holidays on the 19th. At this point, we were very optimistic.

We called Sasha to pick us up and headed to the village and the internot. When we arrived around noon, the village was quiet as was the orphanage. There was a bone chilling wind that made our choice of winter coats a good one.

Nika appeared from the dark entrance to greet us. "Where are Albina and Nadya?" Paula asked looking around.

"Albina is in school and Nadya is in the hospital," Nika replied.

"What happened? Is she okay?" Paula asked.

"We don't know if she is okay. They just took her to the hospital," Nika smiled.

"Where is the hospital?" I asked. "Please take us there."

Nika turned and told Sasha where the hospital was located and he drove us. There are no doctors in the village so whenever one of the kids gets sick, they go directly to the hospital which is located just a couple of blocks from the orphanage

When we entered, it was like stepping back in time. I recently saw the movie *Fly Boys* about World War I fighter pilots and there is a scene where one of the guys was in a field hospital. This could have been that hospital.

Inside it was very dark and on by the entrance was a room with five nurses sitting, talking and laughing. Vitaly asked them where Nadya was and they pointed to the first room on the left. I opened the curtain to see Nadya lying in bed flanked by two women in their mid 70's. She smiled broadly when she saw Paula and got out of bed to join us in the hallway.

She had a fever and showed us the lymph nodes on either side of her neck that were swollen the size of walnuts. They were rough and she said that she felt very bad but would be better soon.

"I am sick. Do you still want to adopt me?" Nadya said. "I can come to America for Christmas. I will be better, the doctor says I will be better."

We assured her that we would still adopt her even if she were sick. It didn't matter to us at all. "We just want you to get well," Paula said. "We will talk to the doctor and see what is going on."

I asked Vitaly to find the doctor so we could speak to him but he came back and said, "He is not here. He is gone for the day. We can see him tomorrow at noon when he comes back to see his patients. He is the only doctor for 14 village hospitals and very busy."

Sasha had brought Nadya a Snickers candy-bar, not exactly what she needed at the moment, so Paula politely asked him to keep it and give it to one of his own children. He didn't understand but went along with us and put it in his pocket.

"We'll be back to see how you're doing tomorrow and talk to the doctor. You get some more rest, ok?" I said. "We're sure everything will work out just fine"

Nadya's face lit up and for the first time you could see she felt safe and special — truly special.

We decided to check on the school and see what time Albina would get out because we were sure she hadn't yet heard that the SDA had given us permission to adopt her and we couldn't wait any longer to tell her.

**The school at the orphanage**

Albina got out of class at exactly 1 p.m. and we were standing in the parking lot waiting for her.

"Mama, Papa," she yelled running towards us with her arms outstretched. We told her how sorry we were about leaving for Cleveland after the SDA had turned us down, and how they said it would be ok now.

"We are so happy," Paula said.

The weather at the orphanage was deteriorating quickly so we moved inside the main building to see some of the other kids who were watching their favorite TV drama's exported from the U.S. The shows were not age-appropriate but the children watched whatever the supervising teacher wanted to watch.

I looked around the room and noticed that my little friend King Arthur was nowhere to be found so I asked Nika who said, "Oh, he is very sick and in the hospital," but that's all she knew. I never did find out what happened to him. The children in orphanages sometimes disappear. Arteom, or King Arthur as I called him, meant a lot to me even though we had never said a word to each other. We needed no words. We had a special connection. He needed someone who cared. That's all. Someone who would not pull away and leave him, but embrace him, and shield him from whatever it was that he was afraid of. I was proud to be that someone, if even only for a short time.

*December 11th*
*Melitopol, Ukraine*

Our first order of business was to locate Nadya's brother and grandmother and then come back and see the doctor about Nadya. At this point, all we knew was that Nadya's relatives lived in a small town whose name loosely translated to "Happy Town" and that was some 40 minutes from the orphanage. Valery had given us this information after he tried to talk to the grandmother. She wouldn't even talk about adoption. Not too encouraging but we had to take things one step at a time and this was our first step.

Sasha came early and we dropped by the orphanage to pick up Nadya. Both Nadya and Albina were pretty quiet because they didn't know what we were doing and frankly, we weren't too sure either. We were totally dependent on Vitaly to take charge and tell us what he needed us to do, and when.

"Happy Town" has about 20,000 residents spread out over a large area of well-planted farmland. There is also a small town center surrounding a 50 ft. statue of Lenin (as usual.)

The current problem was that we had no idea where to find Nikolia, Nadya's brother, and her grandmother. I saw this as a big issue, but Vitaly being who he was, told Sasha to stop at a house we were driving by with two older women standing outside. He got out of the car and asked them if they knew the grandmother. One woman pointed down the street and Vitaly hopped back into the car. "She said there is a man that lives about a kilometer from here that might know her so we will go there."

Down the road we went, right turn, left turn, right turn and then we stopped in front of a large apartment building with no doors and a lady pushing a baby carriage and pulling a goat. Vitaly and Sasha disappeared inside and Paula and Nadya waited patiently in the car as I wandered around with my video camera trying to capture this place for future recall. After 20 minutes, I was getting antsy and poked my head in the apartment entrance. Oh boy! I have never smelled anything like it, *worse* than the Donetsk airport restroom. The stench permeated my clothes and I almost ran out the door. I couldn't believe that Vitaly and Sasha could still be in there. What was that smell?

Fifteen more minutes passed and finally they came out and walk directly to the car. I asked, "How could you stand the smell in there?"

Vitaly, deep in thought, just said, "It is not too bad. Any place could smell like this because they do not have toilets and go in the halls."

Then, I asked, "Did you find out anything about the grandmother?"

"Yes, we think there is an uncle who lives not too far from here. We will go there." And we crammed back into the car.

We rode through the farmland on pothole-ridden roads in silence. I was wondering how Sasha could possibly find his way through the maze of roads.

At length, we pulled up in front of a little yellow house with a rusty, broken down old truck parked in the front yard. There was no grass and about five dogs were running in circles around two children playing in the yard (without coats… it was 30 degrees!) Vitaly got out of the car, walked to the door and knocked. A large woman answered the door and they talked for quite awhile.

When Vitaly returned, he said, "She is Nadya's aunt and she said that her grandmother is a couple of kilometers from here living on a farm. We will go there now."

Back through the labrynth of streets we go, leaving the town center and heading back into the country. A mile or so outside of town, Sasha pulled into a farm and a barking dog ran towards us.

I thought, "This is it? This is where Nadya's relatives live." It was an old unpainted shack and there was a tall handsome young man wearing a black leather coat and wool cap pulled tightly over his face standing outside waiting for us. As we pulled in, Nadya was visibly excited and jumped from the car. The young man was her brother Nikolia, about 6'2" and looked just like Brad Pitt, unusual for Ukraine.

Nadya and Nikolia embraced for a long time and then he gave us the once-over. Vitaly introduced us as Nikolia's girlfriend joined by him. They then invited us inside.

Nikolia and his grandmother work on this farm and live in a one-room house about the size of our dining room at home. There were two single beds, a makeshift closet and a TV that I guessed, ran 24 hours a day.

Nadya's grandmother was obviously disturbed that we had come and was very cold to us when we were introduced as the people that wanted to adopt her granddaughter. Paula and I just stood there and smiled as much as we could in this most uncomfortable moment while Vitaly was talking at a hundred miles an hour.

After about five minutes, she started crying and Vitaly turned to us, "She has agreed to allow you to adopt. She says that she knows it will be best for her and she wants Nadya to have a good life." We thanked her as best as we could and then Vitaly started talking to Nikolia who needed to agree not to be adopted and sign a letter acknowledging that we could take his sister.

We also had to ask Nikolia if he wanted to be adopted. Nikolia says, "Yes, I want to be adopted, too."

We knew that this wouldn't be possible and Vitaly told him that we are required to ask him this question because Nadya was still a minor and has been in the orphanage but we really cannot adopt him since he is too old and illiterate. He wouldn't have a chance in the USA at this point in his life.

Nikolia did not understand what was going on, but after playing with Nadya and talking to her privately, she told him that she wanted to come to America and that she needed him to write a letter for her or she cannot go. He was a good brother and realized that this is what is best for his little sister, so he agreed to write the letter. He must also state that he agreed to allow us to separate him from his sister. This has been a hard time for all of us on many levels and we were all conflicted but working towards a greater good.

We stayed at the farmhouse for another 30 minutes, took pictures with Nadya, her brother and grandmother, made plans for the next day to go to the local government office and then leave. Everyone was tired and although happy, we felt that life in Ukraine could and should be easier for its citizens.

Paula, Michael, Nadya, Grandmother, and Nikolia

As with everything we attempted to accomplish in Ukraine, there was always more to the story. There will be several more steps to securing permission from Nikolia starting with the city government organization in charge of him. We needed to ask them for permission to separate the children before he could even write the letter, so on the way out of town, we stopped at city hall which was another building that has seen better days, and Vitaly did his disappearing act again to find the appropriate person returning 30 minutes later.

"This will be easier than I thought," he said. "They will have Nikolia write the letter and then get it signed and stamped right here. We won't need to go to Zaporizhzhya for the letter. We will meet Nikolia here tomorrow and it will be done."

This was a big relief because typically, every paper we filed in Ukraine needed to be signed, notarized, stamped and officially strung together to presented as a package to the SDA.

On the way back to town, we stopped at the hospital to speak with the doctor who was in for a short time making his rounds. When we walked into his office, he seemed surprised to see us even though we had made an appointment with him.

"Can you tell us exactly what is wrong with Nadya?" I asked.

"She has an infection," he says deadpan. "We have run tests and I think she will be better in a couple of days."

"Do we know the cause of this infection?"

"The children at the internot get many infections and most of the time we do not know what they are, or where they came from. Her tests do not show that it is serious," the doctor said as he stood up to leave.

I pushed a little. "When will she leave the hospital?"

"When she is better," he said. "Maybe three or four days."

We left not knowing much more than when we came except that Nadya's illness was not life threatening and we should be able to take her home for Christmas.

That night, Paula and I sat and tried to think of what we might be able to do to help Nikolia. He was 16, illiterate and stuck in the system. He worked on a farm with no future, no guidance and about the only thing we could do for him was buy him a cell phone to keep in touch with his sister, which we did. Oh, did I mention that he was getting married? At sixteen!

*December 12th*
*Happy Town, Ukraine*

The next morning, Paula and I were walking into town on one of the multiple paths that cut through the wooded areas surrounding our hotel and noticed a couple getting their wedding photos taken. What seemed odd to us was that it was only about 20 degrees, she was not wearing a coat, in high heels, and a huge entourage surrounded them. We didn't pay too much attention other than a quick laugh about how people who are so in love they couldn't care less.

We continued our walk and rounded a corner onto the main street and there was another couple in wedding garb taking pictures.

"Wow! What a coincidence, that we would run into two couples the same day," I said. This couple had a professional photographer and the bride was dressed to the nines.

This was our usual daily grocery trip where we stocked up on crackers, yogurt, fruit, veggies, olives, olive oil and maybe some cheese or salami. We left the store before the city was even awake and thought we could catch up on some email and possibly to talk to Grace and June in the lobby of the hotel, so we headed straight back past all of the young men carrying newly-opened bottles of beer the size of small kegs, and local operators opening their stores.

As we walked past the war memorial by our hotel, which every town in Ukraine has, several cars pulled up and guess what? Another wedding party got out of the cars and proceeded to set up for their wedding pictures. This was starting to get bizarre. I mean, when have you been for a short walk and seen three different weddings in 30 minutes? But wait! That's not all — as they say on TV. There was another couple across the street in the memorial park taking wedding pictures in the woods and yet another couple sitting on a swing in the playground — taking photos. Something strange was going on here.

Ukraine as it turns out is rated in the top 10 highest divorce rates on our planet — 3.8 per 1,000. Women in Ukraine need a man to survive economically so they get married as soon as they leave home and in many cases, quit school to get married. While we were in Melitopol, we witnessed over 50 wedding parties and a couple of times they were standing in the snow to get those precious photos.

*December 13th*
*Happy Town, Ukraine*

Paula and I were getting used to all of the very early morning travels, so when Sasha pulled into the hotel driveway at 7:15 a.m., we were already dressed and ready to go. Our plan was to go back to Happy Town without Nadya and get the letters we needed Nikolia to write and sign.

The drive was long but we read our books and napped on the way. When you adopt in a smaller town, you must continually travel back and forth to a regional center like Zaporizhzhya, to get papers signed to continue the process.

When we arrived in Happy Town at the city hall, we climbed four flights of stairs stopping along the way for Vitaly, bothered by his heart arrhythmia and knocked on the door to the small office where the administrator was located. She opened the door, invited us in and again, I just sat and listened. I was used to Vitaly taking charge and the conversation became a blur of low volume unintelligible Russian.

The administrator told us, "I will have the papers ready in a couple of hours."

It was still early and quite cold but there was a small market across the street that looked like it was already open so we strolled for a while. The markets in Ukraine typically have all of the same products but this one had a different spin and focused on cheap warm work clothes. You could buy a pair of boots for $10 and a warm coat for $15. The customers are mostly farmers who have no need for fancy things.

While we were wandering through the market, we spotted a small photo shop tucked behind a building that sold used car parts. We decided to develop the photos we had taken the previous day with Nadya and her grandmother, so we handed them to the shopkeeper. He said he could develop them in one hour for about $2.

Reading this, you can't fully appreciate how strange it was to find this little photo shop in Happy Town — I would have bet against it. He had a PC and a little Kodak photo printer and that was it, but he still had a line of people waiting for his services.

We went back to the administrator's office about two hours later but she had not yet completed the papers and said to come back after lunch. This is how it goes here… you can't really plan anything. That's the reason you are told you will be in country for three to six weeks. Everything depends on procedures, notaries, politics, and money — not necessarily in that order.

We decided it would be best to go get Nikolia, so we took the short drive back to the farmhouse and were told he would be at work, at a factory of some kind. We drove to the factory but he wasn't there. We thought that he must have taken off to avoid us and it was be a big problem all the way 'round. Vitaly, in his infinite wisdom, contacted the administrator who called the police who tracked him down and ultimately brought him to meet us. He told us he had planned to meet us but something had come up. Hmmmm …

Well, at least he was there and very happy to get the cell phone. I explained, "We bought you this cell phone so that you could call your sister whenever you want." We had a quick lunch of a chicken cutlet and coffee and went back to see the administrator.

I really felt like a fly on the wall at this meeting, not understanding a word. Nikolia was questioned in Russian, "Do you want to be adopted?"

"Yes," he said.

"But it is okay if you are not adopted?" Vitaly said.

"Yes, it is okay."

"Can these people, Paula and Michael Redman, adopt your sister Nadya?"

"Yes."

"Then you will need to write a letter to that effect," says the administrator.

Nikolia's face flushed and his gaze fell to the floor. Everything stopped. Nikolia could neither read nor write. He had no real use for it as a labore, he just needed a strong back. The administrator started writing the letter for him.

After a few minutes, the door opened. "Come with me, please," I was told.

"Okay, but why?" I said.

"The Mayor wants to meet you."

"Alright," I said as I followed her down the stairs. What did he want to meet me for? More problems I was guessing.

The Mayor's office was at the end of a long hallway separated from all of the other offices. By this time, I was getting used to everyone questioning us and was ready for another grilling.

To my surprise, when the door opened, a stylish 35-year-old man in a sport suit approached me with his hand outstretched and a big grin on his face. He excitedly welcomed me to his office and in very broken English tried to thank me for visiting him and adopting Nadya. He had never met a person from America and I think he was just curious to see what I would be like. After a few minutes of trying to communicate, we both laughed and bid farewell, but not before he gave me a little document that I think was the equivalent of the key to his city.

I was taken back upstairs where they were still hard at work typing away on the 10-year-old Dell computer and after another about 30 minutes the administrator was finally done. She turned to Nikolia and started reading the document as he listened carefully. When she was finished, he signed the papers and we are once again told that we would need to come back in an hour to pick up the stamped official version.

We took a short walk with Nikolia and his girlfriend, had a cup of instant coffee and one hour later we were happy to leave Happy Town.

*December 15th*
*Zaporizhzhya, Ukraine*

By now, you may be tired of reading the step-by-step, challenge-by-challenge account of our journey but I am writing this book/journal as an abbreviated version of the actual day-to-day events. Our trip was actually much more involved, but it would simply be too tedious for me to write or for you to read.

The most important thing I hope you take away from this account of our adoption is that you must remain strong, committed, and give up control — because you will not have any in Ukraine. So, relax and be as open to it as you can.

Off to Zaporizhzhya at 8 a.m. with a new driver, Henry, with the goal of meeting Albina's 16-year-old sister, Veronica, and have her write a letter refusing to be adopted as well as consent to our adoption of Albina — just like Nikolia. Vitaly has found through his research that she is no longer in an orphanage and that she attends a local vocational school learning to be a construction painter.

Our first stop was at the Zaporizhzhya inspector's office to obtain permission to visit Veronica and talk to her about splitting up the siblings. We had driven two and a half hours to Zaporizhzhya, and entered yet another large, old building under renovation. The design of the new floor tile they were installing looked like it was from the 1950s. I wondered what it would look like when they were finished [maybe 1960]. Sitting outside the inspector's office, I wished I had brought a copy of *Great Expectations* or any other 1,500+ page book so the waiting might pass a little quicker. We would sit there for two hours before the inspector finally saw us. Vitaly was summoned behind a door with a simple scrap of paper with the inspector's name and title taped to it.

Thirty minutes later Vitaly comes out with a frown on his face (he looked like he had practiced this frown for years because it was perfect) and tells us, "She says come back at 2:30 today because she does not have time to see us now."

By this time, Paula and I were so used to this modus operandi that we were not fazed in the least. "Well, let's go get a good lunch then." Paula said. "And not fast food or pizza."

We headed down the street and somehow ended up in a pizza joint — go figure. At promptly 2:30 p.m., we returned to the inspector's office and Vitaly disappeared again, only to return an hour later, this time with his great big frown and said, "She will not go with us to see the girl [Veronica] today. She said to come back tomorrow at 9:00 a.m. and she will send someone with us."

So another day wasted, another two-and-a-half hour drive back to Melitopol, another drive to the orphanage, and another $75 (cheap, Ochin cheap) cab fare…

"It's Ukraine."

*December 16th*
*Zaporizhzhya, Ukraine*

To make it to Zaporizhzhya by 9 a.m. this morning we would have be on the road by 6:30 a.m and drive fast. So promptly at 6:30, there was a knock at our door. Vitaly called out, "Are you ready? It is time to go, we must leave now!"

He asked because most of the time we weren't ready. Paula and I dozed and read books the whole drive to Zaporizhzhya trying not to bother Vitaly with our endless questions and strategies to get this deal done. We were sure he was as tired of all of this as we were. So the silence was golden.

At 9 a.m., we entered a parking lot by a small outside market that had not opened yet and waited for the official to join us. She turned out to be a pleasant woman in her mid-40s who seemed to sympathize with our situation and circumstances. We drove the short distance to the school and were escorted right to the director's office where we met a neatly dressed man who looked like he was probably a party member 40 years ago and talked like one, too.

All of us sat exactly where he told us and squirmed in our chairs. After a few minutes, they brought Veronica in. She was a 5' 5", 16-year-old with dyed black hair and didn't look very happy. She also didn't look at all like Albina with her hearty build and strong Slavic features. Her face lit up when she saw Albina though and they hugged each other for a long time before settling into chairs to await the subject of this meeting.

As usual Vitaly, the director, and the inspector started talking and Paula and I were in the dark not understanding a word they were saying, but we knew where the conversation was leading. They were asking Veronica if she wanted to be adopted. She responded, "Da." Again, lots of talking. Then there were tears — lots of tears from Veronica, and Albina stood and walked out of the room with her. The inspector followed, as we sat in silence with the director staring right through us and feeling extremely uncomfortable.

Time seemed to be moving in slow motion so I asked director a series of questions through Vitaly about the school, students, weather; anything I could think of. After a few minutes, he started to warm up and even cracked a smile. It became obvious to me that he had two very distinct personalities, the official and the human being.

When I would ask him about anything to do with his personal feelings like a subject about living in Zaporizhzhya, he was candid and friendly, but when the subject turned to the school, his face became stoic, his eyes focused and the smile disappeared as he answered like the government official he was. In all my years, I have never encountered someone like him before. He could turn it on and off like a faucet. You could tell that he was a complex man and although a socialist, he was making the transition to the new paradigm in Ukraine.

When Veronica and Albina returned about a half an hour later, there were more tears but they had come to an agreement. Veronica would write the refusal and consent letters, which only took a short time. It was also suggested by the inspector that we should buy her a cell phone to stay in touch with Albina like Nikolia, so we packed into the car, drove to a local market and bought her a simple phone and phone card, so that Albina could call Veronica anytime via Skype from her new home in the U.S. All of this helped Veronica feel better, and we told her we would also try to work it out so she could come to the U.S. to visit us during the summer.

**Albina, Veronica and Vitaly**

After completing the paperwork for Veronica, we had lunch together and Veronica started to open up. You could see the admiration that Albina had for her sister in the way she looked at her.

Upon leaving the restaurant, we dropped by the inspector's office and the documents were prepared quickly. Vitaly told us he would have to come back to Zaporizhzhya one more time after speaking to Svetlana in Melitopol to get the approval to split the siblings. Finally, we were back in the car and driving to Melitopol for a quick walk, a quick meal, a quick movie on the computer and sleep.

*December 18th*
*Zaporizhzhya, Ukraine*

Another day of running around for Vitaly as he tried desperately to get the SDA papers from the orphanage but to no avail. The orphanage attorney did not complete them and said, "I sent the papers off and am still waiting for the city inspector in Zaporizhzhya to write me."

Vitaly replied and told her, "You are doing a bad job and need to get off you're a@# and take them by hand."

Not too tactful but the point was made I guess. Vitaly then took the girls to the hospital and to the local doctor for their medical exam. Nothing negative turned up and he brought the girls over to our hotel to visit. The day progressed uneventfully thank goodness. We said goodbye to the girls and packed our bags to catch the train back to Kiev and head home.

We also heard from Vitaly that Nadya's grandmother and uncle stormed into Valery's office; both of them stone drunk — and really gave him a hard time. It was a sad situation and Valery threw them out. It's also possible that the grandmother may show up at the court hearing and cause some trouble for us, but it should be apparent by her appearance in front of the judge, that she is an alcoholic. I knew that Nadya loved her very much and we surely didn't want to cause her any trouble, so we were hoping she didn't drink on the day of our court hearing.

By now I have told you many times about the 12-hour train trip from Melitopol to Kiev so let's skip the details and just say that we started the journey home to host the girls for the holidays. We said our goodbyes to Vitaly and Sasha and boarded the train.

# Home for the Holidays

*December 19th*
*Kiev, Ukraine*

The brakes squealed and the train came to a halt early in Kiev where we were met by Dima's driver, Nikolia, and were whisked off to the airport. When we arrived, there were about 80 small children ranging in ages from six to twelve in a very tightly organized line waiting to get their passports checked. No doubt, they were on their way to spend the holidays in America where their lives would be changed forever.

Looking into the eyes of these children you could sense the fear, excitement, anticipation, trepidation and every other emotion that might be tied to being a six-year-old orphan traveling to another country and a different world, where all the rich people live.

Before boarding the plane, I received one last call from Vitaly to give me the latest update which included Albina's sister Veronica's desire to meet them in *Zaporizhzhya*, and travel with the girls on the train to Kiev to catch their flight to visit us. I agreed to pay her fare, which was only $50, as Albina would miss her sister and it would be the last time she would see her for a long, long time. Vitaly also told me that the orphanage attorney didn't complete the papers as promised, thus putting off the submission of our final adoption papers to the SDA once again. We did however have faith that everything would eventually come together and we weren't worried.

*December 20th*
*Kiev, Ukraine*

Aerosvit Airlines brought back vivid memories of the state of the Russian airline industry in 1997 when Paula and I first traveled with her parents to Moscow. Our plane, a 767, was huge but we were packed like sardines and the seating was a free-for-all. Every empty space on the plane was quickly taken up by someone hoping to sleep their way to America.

It was a long haul and with little sleep, we arrived at JFK where I kissed Paula goodbye and put her on the connecting flight to Cleveland. I stayed with our friends Jeff and Judy in midtown and would come back to JFK the next day to meet up with Albina and Nadya and the rest of the hosted children and take them to Cleveland.

Jeff and Judy are a couple of our closest, dearest friends and live right on the river in midtown Manhattan. They have a beautiful 14-year-old adopted daughter, Joanna, and we were able to spend a little time together and have a nice dinner at one of their favorite Italian restaurants right around the corner from their apartment. After dinner, I realized just how exhausted I was from the preceding months in Ukraine and slept hard in what we call "The Mcelnea Hotel."

About 11 a.m., I wished Jeff, Judy and Joanna a Merry Christmas and headed back to JFK after doing a little shopping on 5th Avenue. You can't really come to NYC during the holidays and not shop just a little.

When the cab dropped me off at the airport, it was snowing like crazy. That wet nasty kind of snow, the snow with the *really* big snowflakes. It took me a while, but I finally found the right terminal. I met a couple of other potential fathers waiting to pick up their hosted children as well. I was supposed to meet a representative from Frontier Horizon but received a call that she was stuck in Roanoke, Virginia, as a result of the storm that was creeping up the East Coast so we all just waited.

The girls were to arrive at JFK at about 2:30 p.m. and we figured that we would see them about 3:30 p.m. after they had cleared customs but, "It's Ukraine" had followed us all the way back to America.

The delays started as I waited with the other guys for three and a half hours by the escalator the girls were to come up after clearing customs. I stood and glanced down the steps about every 15 seconds to see if our group was on their way. Let me see, that would be some 840 times. Maybe that's why I had a headache.

At about 7 p.m., I noticed the guard was closing the heavy metal doors at the bottom of the escalator. We had all missed our connecting flights home by this time and what made it ridiculous was that we had no idea where our children were.

Another 45 minutes go by and we are asking security, attendants and whoever would listen, "Have you seen 60 Ukrainian kids?" Nope? No? Of course not.

It was not one of the highlights of our trip as I frantically ran around the airport looking for the girls. We couldn't go too far in any direction because they might come out another door and we would miss them. I didn't have anybody's cell phone number either, and no one had mine — so this was *the* train wreck. The snowstorm had shut down most of the East Coast and flights were being cancelled and delayed by the hundreds.

Suddenly, I spotted the girls on the other side of the security glass in line with at least 1,000 other people waiting to go through the general security line. They had shut down the customs exit and sent the children outside into the snow to re-enter the airport.

Vincent [the director of Frontier Horizon] was waving to me to come through the secure doors and into the security line and I was saying, "NO! NO! If I come in I'll have to wait for hours with everybody. There must be some other way."

Finally I gave in, opened the door and crossed the line into the crowd of angry stranded airline passengers only to have 50 people yelling at me for butting in line to be with my girls. By that time, I had hit bottom emotionally and didn't care one bit what they said. I wasn't leaving!

Vincent hastily handed me a package of tickets and passports for the girls and said, "Hi Mike, it's nice to meet you.

Here are your girls. Take good care of them. BYE!" and he disappeared into the masses.

Behind me a man saw our dilemma and said, "Hey, go to the front of the line and talk to the security guy. He might let you through." I thanked him, grabbed the girl's hands and plowed my way to the front of the security line. It was the first time I had ever done something like that and now I understand the desperation some people face when they are stranded and trying to get home.

Once we reached the front of the security checkpoint, I addressed the security officer, "Excuse me, Excuse me, our plane is taking off in five minutes!"

He responded, "You'll have to get a Delta representative to get you through."

I looked around and saw no one that remotely resembled a Delta employee and figured that we were done. That's it! We'll spend the night in a hotel and hope for the best tomorrow.

All of a sudden I heard a lady screaming behind me, "Make way, please! Coming through!"and when I turned, there she was, the Delta rep with her hand pointing straight at the ceiling and the other hand dragging two people through the security line.

"These people need to get through right away," she said to the security guy, and he immediately opened the gate.

Opportunity only strikes once in a great while and when it does you need to be ready, so I grabbed the girls and said, "Quick, follow those people!" and we fell in line right behind them.

The security guy saw us and kind of looked the other way but then 50 more people behind us tried to do the same thing. The security guard jumped in front of the, hands raised and yelling, "Get back in line! Get back in line"

Time seemed to come to a standstill as we waited for our bags to come through the x-ray machine, clock ticking and our plane departing in less than five minutes. When our bags finally appeared, we grabbed them, put on our shoes and I motioned to the girls to run. I wish I had the words and time to explain but it was one of those, "Oh, hell!" moments.

I tried to grab the girls' backpacks to no avail. Albina and Nadya could see the stress on my face and decided it would be best to carry them. Off we went at a dead run to the other side of Terminal 3 which is about one-half mile away. The girls stayed with me stride for stride, and I thought my heart was going to pop right out of my chest.

At every corner I thought we had made it, only to see another people mover stretching out for miles before us. On and on we went until we reached Gate 19. I looked up, barely breathing, and the airport monitor no longer even said, 'Cleveland.' It now read 'Flint, Michigan.' The wind left my sails hanging empty, and I gave in as I asked for confirmation from the busy, frowning gate attendant, "Cleveland is gone, right?"

"No, it's not even here yet," she said continuing to frown. But, I couldn't help but smile. We made it… but the night was still young.

Ten minutes after settling in at the gate I looked down towards Albina who was tired and staring blankly at the floor and something terribly was wrong. Nadya was gone! I frantically scanned the gate area and up and down the surrounding gates but no Nadya. Panic-struck, I thought she might have been picked up by a stranger and taken to who knows where.

I ran to the left about five gates and returned to tell Albina to stay where she was while I looked for Nadya. She was perfectly content, exhausted from her 30-hour trip. Just then a woman who was walking by asks, "Are you looking for the other girl? I was on the plane from Kiev with them."

"Yes," I said.

"I saw her on the way to the other terminal," she replied.

I could not believe it as I ran again towards Terminal B passing thousands of weary travelers and scouring the crowd as I went, looking for any sign of Nadya. Nothing… I ran further, nothing.

I saw a little blond girl who was going into the restroom. "That's her," I thought to myself and yelled, "Nadya! Nadya!" she stopped and spun around. It was not Nadya.

Turning a corner nearly one-half mile from our gate I finally saw Nadya. She was at the far end of the terminal on the moving walkway, walking quickly, head down and not looking back. I yelled, "Nadya!" once and then again but she was too far away to hear. I ran faster, "Nadya!" I screamed hoping she would hear me over the crowd and before she could disappear.

She finally looked back and I was waving my arms and yelling like a madman, "Nadya!" She saw me and slowed down but didn't stop. I ran faster, catching her as she rounded the last corner that leaves the terminal.

"What are you doing? Where are you going?" I said exasperated, knowing full well she didn't understand a word I was saying. She just smiled a funny little smile, looked up at me and grabbed my hand. We turned and jogged almost a mile back to the gate where Albina was waiting for us and confused passengers were still milling around the gate.

The first indication that we might get out of New York was an updated display on the monitor for a Cleveland departure at 9:15 p.m. That was fine with us after all we had been through. We would be home by 11 p.m., not bad — but the status display kept changing — 9:55, then 10:30, 11:15, 12:20 a.m. We were very tired but happy to board at 12:30 a.m.

As in the commercials you sometimes see, "But, that's not all folks, there's more."

The pilot comes on and tells us, "No need to worry everybody, my crew is on duty until 4:30 a.m. so we'll get you home tonight or early in the morning." I was relieved until he continued, "We just need to find some fuel, so if we can find a refueling truck at this time of night we'll be in good shape. Once we locate one, we'll refuel and get de-iced one more time before I get you up in the air and on your way home."

Two hours later at 2:30 a.m., we refueled, the girls were asleep and although my legs were starting to cramp, I knew it was only a matter of time before we were actually airborne. Then, a final message from the cockpit, "Sorry for all of these delays folks but I would like everybody to look out the windows on the left side of our aircraft. See that plane way out there on the runway ... your luggage is on that plane! Welcome to JFK! The good news is that they haven't left yet and we will get your luggage. It will just be a little bit more of a delay."

Unbelievable! That's JFK.

We arrived in Cleveland at 4:45 a.m. and home at 6:20 a.m., but at least we were home for the holiday when so many of the other poor souls we saw at the airport were not, including most of the kids from Ukraine and their hosting families.

*December 21st*
*Chagrin Falls, Ohio*

As we walked in, the girls were welcomed by a sleepy-eyed Grace who had been waiting a long, long time for this moment, and not very patiently. Nadya stared at Grace, and Grace stared back for almost 15 minutes, both trying to understand each other on some level that a father can never know. Albina was already busy arranging her bedroom, the first she has ever had.

I can't remember when I've been so exhausted and I took a shower while all of the introductions were being made.

Our first afternoon home, we took the girls to a concert at Federated Church which backs up to the beautiful Chagrin River and we listened to the famous Cleveland Jazz Orchestra as they moved through a set of traditional and not-so-traditional holiday music. Paula's mother had called the church ahead of time and arranged for two pews for the entire family who arrived just as the music began. All of the cousins and parents smiled and greeted Albina and Nadya not knowing exactly what to say and the girls looking somewhat confused smiled back at everyone with a sparkle in their eyes.

The music set the tone for the holidays and I felt a flood of emotion come over me as I looked at our new family and the family I had inherited some 17 years ago. God has always led me in this direction and I felt at home — comfortable and loved. I smiled at Paula and she gave me a hug. We knew that the page had turned and a new life was beginning for us.

Our holiday continued with a family dinner at the Hunt Club, one of the oldest in Cleveland and as the name implies, a horse club. Most of the members have and love horses, and tonight they had a special room for the seventeen members of the Ames family with a roaring fire, a beautiful eight-foot Christmas tree. The attentive staff delivered large plates of hors d'oeuvres and Nadya, standing close to me, asked, "What are these? I'll eat lots of them." I just laughed, sure that she thought she was in heaven and that this was her dinner.

The night was filled with joy and stories of our journey, which unknown to us, was far from over.

*December 23rd*
*Chagrin Falls, Ohio*

I awoke to little laughing voices that sounded like they were coming from another planet. Sleepy-eyed, I wandered downstairs trying to figure out what I was hearing and as I entered the kitchen got my answer. The girls had discovered the computer, the Internet and the *games2girls* website. All three girls were playing some game with strange characters jumping around, and they were hypnotized.

There are very few computers in the orphanage world they came from and this was the first time Albina and Nadya had ever seen one that was working, so playing a game for them was over the top. In fact, when Paula and I first toured the orphanage with Valery, he proudly took us into the library that had row after row of desks with computer monitors. Upon closer inspection we noticed that none of them were hooked up to anything. The monitor cables dangled to the floor and were not plugged in ; there were no computers, just the monitors.

Once breakfast was over, I reintroduced the girls to the computer and explained to them that the most important thing for them to do while they were with us over the holidays was to start learning English. The Rosetta Stone language program was to be one of the best investments we ever made and I showed the girls how simple it would be to listen to the lady's voice, look at a picture and then repeat the words. They spent 30 minutes every day working with the program and it wasn't long until a few English words started flowing from them.

Along with the English lessons, we purchased some movies in Russian to make them more comfortable, and located a Russian deli/grocer a few miles away in Mayfield Heights. It was fun to see some of the same food we enjoyed in Melitopol available at our local grocery store and took home a variety of soups, salamis and salads.

Last minute Christmas shopping was an understatement this year. Paula and I had one day to shop for the girls and Tyler [my son] and the list was long. At the top of the list were bikes because at the orphanage there were only six bikes used exclusively by the teachers, so as much as the children wanted to ride one, it wasn't an option. Target proved to be the place to shop this year and I purchased two bikes, pajamas, DVDs, music, and a few other things. Christmas would be about family this year with only a few presents. It would not be a gift fest.

We didn't want to send the wrong message to Nadya and Albina about Christmas and what it meant.

We didn't get around to putting up the Christmas tree until the evening of the 23$^{rd}$. I built a big fire in the fireplace, flooded the house with Christmas music and Paula made apple cider and kid-friendly snacks. Nadya almost single-handedly decorated the tree as we sat and sang Christmas carols together. It was a good night.

*December 24th*
*Chagrin Falls, Ohio*

Home, a roaring fire in the fireplace, a new snowfall blanketing our back yard, 29 degrees, happy faces full of wonder, a walk in town to see the lights, thankfulness.

**Our home in Chagrin Falls, Ohio**

*December 25th*
*Chagrin Falls, Ohio*

In our house, we have a tradition of getting up at the regular waking time Christmas morning somewhere around 7 a.m., and do our Christmas gift exchange, which takes place after a leisurely breakfast. Albina and Nadya had never experienced Christmas so we were able to keep to this tradition intact without much problem, although I am sure that they had sifted through all the presents prior to our getting up.

It was one of those perfect Midwest Christmas mornings with a light steady snow falling from the heavens and a frosty 27 degrees when Paula's parents Chuck and Jay dropped in to join us about 8:30 a.m. We had a nice fire going, coffee, tea, and a few gifts under the tree to welcome them.

Front and center under the tree was a shiny new purple 21-speed mountain bike with Nadya's name on it and was she beside herself! Propping up the bike were two scooters and various other presents for the girls from friends and relatives. With beautiful Christmas music playing in the background, Paula and I sat and watched our children open their presents, hoping this may someday become their own tradition.

For the rest of Christmas day, we hung out and enjoyed each other — the girls rode their bikes and scooters in the snow and Paula and I recuperating from our journey. The days' festivities continued well into the night as we gathered up our family and drove across town to Shaker Heights to Christmas dinner at Cindy's house. Cindy, Paula's younger sister, is a ball of energy and is not happy when she's not juggling multiple balls at the same time. Tonight was no exception. She had a full house, and tables for 25 or so guests. I think I saw her for maybe 10 minutes the entire night as she was running past me hugging everyone in her path on her way to take care of somebody or something. She truly is an amazing woman and such an asset to the family.

Albina and Nadya spent time playing with their new cousins. Even with the language barrier, they spoke, laughed, ate and had a great time. It was so incredible to watch the children accept and be accepted by their new family. I can only imagine the types of things they must have been thinking. What would it be like to be a child and move to another country where you didn't speak the language and where you had a new family, in unfamiliar surroundings? It must have been a very scary at times for our girls, and we were watching closely to make sure they didn't get overwhelmed

*December 26th*
*Chagrin Falls, Ohio*

The next morning with the temperature dropping and the thermometer barely tipping 15 degrees, the girls took to the snowy street on their bikes and scooters to be joined by our neighbor Katie, for a quick tour of our neighborhood which is also a bit of a drag strip for the local 16-yr-old drivers. It was slightly unnerving but they were safe enough. What amazed me was how Grace, Nadya, and Albina could spend two hours riding bikes and rolling in the wet snow and not be bothered by any of it. I guess I've forgotten what it was like to have that fire burning in a strong, young body.

While the girls were busy, I ducked out to visit Starbucks only to run into four friends with too many questions about the adoption to answer. I think I was still in a daze, because they all asked me why I had such big bags under my eyes.

Later that evening we all decided to go to a movie. Nadya and Albina had never been to a theater before. June said, "I heard that *Marley and Me* is good," I agreed and we headed out for the 5 p.m. showing. Boy, was that a mistake!

I've had my privilege of picking movies taken away from me by Paula for some time now because I have, on occasion, picked a loser. Well this was another one ... I thought it would be a nice family movie about a dog. As it turned out, there was sex, fear, tough language, and to top it off, *[spoiler alert!]* the dog dies! I agreed with Paula that I should move into the doghouse when I got home. Paula decided that she would pick the movies from now on.

After the movie Albina was very sad. We were unable to communicate that it was just a movie, a bad choice, and that the dog didn't really die.

*December 27th*
*Chagrin Falls, Ohio*

A really special day as two of our closest friends, Vic and Joan Gelb, recommended and were able to secure five prime tickets to the Rockettes Christmas Special at the Cleveland Playhouse Theater. The girls all took off downtown for a day of entertainment with The Rockettes.

My son Tyler and I just strolled around Chagrin Falls. All he wanted for Christmas was my used Apple G5 Power Tower, so we spent part of the day cleaning off the hard drive and took it to FedEx who were happy to pack and ship it to his home in Florida. A great deal at $35 — much better than the "Pack and Ship" UPS stores who wanted to charge us $200 for the same service.

Tyler had not said much about us adopting the girls, although I believe from his actions, that he was in favor of it. He likes playing with them and is very secure with himself.

*December 28 th*
*Chagrin Falls, Ohio*

Tyler headed back to Florida and his mom and the girls were very unhappy to see him go. So was I. Tyler is their big brother now and their best playmate, tossing them around in the basement for hours on end. He'll make an exceptional father someday even though he says he'll never have children.

Our next week together passed in a flurry of activities that included introducing our Ukrainian guests to sushi, hiking in the vast network of The Cleveland Metro Parks, sledding, visiting the wonderful Great Lakes Science Center, more biking and endless games.

**Albina, Nadya and Grace**

Everyday, the girls would spend their 30 minutes on the Rosetta Stone program learning more English and asking, "When do we have to go back to the orphanage?" A hard question that we tried to answer in as gentle a way as possible, as we could see the days passing quickly, too.

# The Final Trip

*January 7th, 2009*
*Chagrin Falls, Ohio*

**Blog Entry** - Okay, we are still at it. Paula leaves tomorrow for Ukraine & Melitopol to take the girls back after the holidays. We have had a wonderful time with some ups and downs, language problems and misunderstandings ... but all in all - a grand time.

Albina and Nadya want to be American Girls (so what's new.)  It is amazing to watch.

I will follow Paula on Sunday and hopefully we can have court quickly. Please stay tuned, as I am sure there will be some additional strange things that happen from this point on.

Talk to you soon
Michael

*January 7th*
*Chagrin Falls, Ohio*

We hoped today would not arrive so quickly as it is the end of our holiday hosting with Nadya and Albina. We are off to Cleveland Hopkins Airport and everybody is kind of quiet. Paula and I are trying to keep things light but it is obvious that the girls are not happy about going back to Melitopol. They simply don't want to go back to the orphanage and they think we might leave them there because, at this point, their future is still up in the air. We don't know how everything will turn out with the SDA either, federal laws prohibiting adopting non-related siblings, natural siblings, and a long list of other possible problems we cannot even imagine at this point.

Paula is taking the girls back to Kiev and I am to follow in a couple of days.

Grace and I said our goodbyes to the girls and it was an emotional parting for me. Once again, I will be separated from my wife, and the girls will be left in limbo — not knowing what would happen to them. It was a very tough day.

Their trip, for the most part, was uneventful. Flights were on schedule and Dima met Paula and the girls in Kiev and put them on the night train to Melitopol with only a few hours delay.

In a blink of an eye it was almost time for me to leave.

*January 9th*
*Chagrin Falls, Ohio*

I asked Grace if she wanted me to tell Mom anything and she just said, "Tell her I miss her." Grace is growing up so fast in this crazy little world of ours.

It was just four months ago that Paula was traveling back and forth to New York going to school to get her nutritional certification and Grace would go into a fit crying for her Mom for hours on end… that has all changed. She is much more secure and knows Paula is coming back to her. Grace said, "Tell Mom to tell the girls that I miss them and want them to come back soon and be my sisters." A very telling statement.

June will arrive once again, to take on the formidable task of raising Grace for the next few weeks. I checked on her flight from Tampa to Cleveland — it was on time at 9:30 a.m. so the plan was good. By 10 a.m. her flight had been canceled! This was probably the result of the current sagging economy as well as flights being less full. It seemed that airlines cancel flights with no explanation.

Things got a little crazier when I decided to check my flight to JFK and it was canceled, too! I thought to myself, "This is surely some kind of omen." But since I don't believe in omens and don't think God sits around playing with peoples' travel plans either, I blew it off. I called Cindy, our angelic travel agent, who was able to reschedule June on a 4 p.m. flight even though the airlines automatically moved her to a flight three days later. She reworked my flight as well and in a matter of a few hours, everything was back on track again.

At 8pm, Grace and I drove to Akron-Canton Regional Airport to pick up June and the snow was coming down so hard it was like a nighttime whiteout. June was chipper after her flight and Grace was starving as usual, so we stopped and had a quick bite to eat, then home and off to bed shortly after packing. Yes, I am the stereotypical male and pack at the last moment possible for a trip. It took me about 20 minutes to stuff some warm clothes and all of the electronics I carry into one suitcase.

```
Blog Entry - Paula, Albina, and Nadya
headed back to Ukraine yesterday after a
very nice holiday.  The girls were upset
and never wanted to go back but we must now
continue the process which we are hopeful
will go this way:

1. I travel to Ukraine on Sunday.
2. Vitaly meets the judge in Melitopol on
   Monday to set the court date for Tuesday
   or Wednesday.
3. We will go to court and the judge will
   approve the adoption of both girls.
4. Paula will come home and relieve June who
   has been a real trouper taking care of
```

our eight-year-old Grace. If you decide to do this, you will need some papers for one parent to complete this process.

5. Vitaly and I will travel to Zaporizhzhya and everywhere in the region to collect the rest of the papers and passports for the girls.

6. Travel to Kiev for an appointment with the U.S. Embassy.

7. Get the visas, etc. from the Embassy.

8. Bring the girls home.

9. Try to forget the bad parts of our four-month journey to Ukraine.

Well, that's the plan anyway-stay tuned and we'll see how it actually turns out:)
MR

*January 10th*
*Chagrin Falls, Ohio*

As I have said over and over, I am truly blessed to have a business that allows me to travel for extended periods of time and can't imagine what most fathers who are adopting must go through. Over the past few weeks, I have taken considerable time arranging a communication plan with my business associates and feel pretty comfortable that all of my current projects and jobs will progress smoothly.

My journey continued again as I boarded my first short flight to Cincinnati, then JFK with only a one-hour connection, which is pretty tight given the travel time between the Domestic and International terminals.

As we touchdown at JFK, we stopped on the runway. The pilot's voice booms over the distorted intercom system, "Great news, everybody. We arrived 30 minutes early because of a big tail wind."

I thought, "This is great. I'll have plenty of time." Wrong again!

The pilot then continues, "Unfortunately we'll have to wait out here on the runway because there's an aircraft at our gate and we won't be allowed to park until 4:30 p.m."

"Oh, well," I thought, getting used to this new age of travel. But, at 4:50, I started to sweat, not really wanting to spend the day and night in New York waiting for another flight, eat crappy hotel food, watch a TV movie and deal with a 5 a.m. wakeup call. Then without warning, we slowly moved toward the gate, only to stop about five yards short.

"We'll need to be towed into this gate," the pilot announced. Thanks for your patience."

I didn't have much patience left, but managed to sit still and ask the attendant if I could move forward to make the now all too familiar "JFK run."

We finally pull into the gate at 5:15 p.m. and I ran like a crazy man to the gate for the flight to Kiev, which was fortunately closer than I had previously thought. They were closing the doors but to my amazement, reopened them to let me in. I haven't seen that in years but maybe they called ahead or something. I didn't care and I wasn't asking questions. Anyway, I made my 5:30pm flight to Kiev, settled into my aisle seat, had a glass of wine and then stayed up all night unable to sleep while writing this chapter.

I arrived safely and on time in Kiev at 7:30 a.m. where I was met by our driver, Nikolia, and whisked off to the train station to once again wait… wait… wait… for nine hours… for a train. I was glad to see Dima standing outside the train station and we spent the next couple of hours planning the stay before I told him, "It's time for you to go. There is no sense in your waiting here all day with me. I can get on the train just fine."

"Are you sure?" he said. "I will take you to the platform and make sure you will be alright before I leave," which he did and said goodbye, until we return with the girls to process them out of the country.

It's funny how everything looks so easy and familiar in another country until your escort leaves you on your own. As soon as Dima left, I stared at the train schedule and the words turned to gibberish, which did nothing but add to my anxiety about finding the right platform and the right train.

Dima had been gone only a couple of hours but the words on the blinking wall schedule no longer made sense and it looked like my departure platform had changed as well. With over an hour until the train would arrive I started comparing an old train ticket to the ever-changing LED wall schedule. Finally, I found Melitopol but, just as I thought, they were trying to fool me! Melitopol was not 'Melitopol' it was spelled "Herennopalia". They were using the name of the city, as it was before Perestroika in the early '80s.

# Court

*January 12th*
*Melitopol, Ukraine*

When my train arrived in Melitopal at 5:30 a.m., I was coming off another semi-sleepless night and really dragging. It was so nice to see Vitaly standing in the cold on the platform waiting for me as usual at the train depot. Sasha was with him and they drove me straight to the Seven Stars where Paula was still sleeping.

I kissed her on the cheek. She crawled out of bed, got dressed and an hour later we submitted our petition for our court date only to be told that they didn't like the format of our documents, and the height and width of the paper. Vitaly spent the rest of the day retyping the petition and getting the appropriate signatures and required stamps.

**Blog Entry** - My trip this time to Melitopol was uneventful as Delta only canceled two flights and lost my luggage. We are getting used to the "It's Ukraine" philosophy. Another 42-hr trip that I survived although I'm quite tired.

After I was functional again, we took a trip to the orphanage and saw Albina. We took a new translator (Sveta) with us to talk about girls' stuff, and met with her caregiver. The caregiver answered a few questions and then could not wait to get out of there.

Valery, in his ever-friendly fashion, roped us into a few more shots of cognac and promised to go with us to Zaporizhzhya to help expedite the passports.

We then asked if Albina would go and find Nadya, and to our amazement, she told us that Nadya was in the hospital! Sometimes here you do not get information unless you ask a direct question. Well, as it turns out, Nadya has a bad throat infection and will be in the local hospital for six days. We have tried to see the doctor but he is not around very much. I am working and hope to get my luggage back with my long underwear and hat, and then out the orphanage.

And YES - it is very cold here!

*January 13th*
*Melitopol, Ukraine*

Another day wasted but we resubmitted the petition with an expedition payment. The process of payola in Ukraine was not only accepted, it was expected.

In our case, as you will find throughout Ukraine, there was a system of payments that can be made for a variety of things from medical care, to legal matters, to speeding tickets. In the case of adoption, the judge can make the court date up to three months from the date of the petition. He also knows that the adopting couple not only want to get home quickly, they need to, so for a fee, you can have your court date moved up.

We met with the judge's assistant and also told her we wanted to have him wave the 10-day official waiting period after the court decree was awarded. The assistant pointed to a car in the dirt parking lot in front of the courthouse and told us, "Go get in that car and wait for a man. It will cost $2,500 cash." So we went out to the car and got in.

Then, a large man approached us, opened the door and sat down. "Put the money in here," he said, as he opened a magazine. Next, he slowly drove out of the parking lot and around the corner.

"Get out," he said, and then drove off, leaving us in the street.

We were told about 30 minutes later that our court date will be the very next day at exactly 10 a.m. and *"Do not be one minute late!"*

We spent the rest of the day going to the market, picking up some yogurt and fruit as usual and ate at my favorite little pizza place.

In Melitopol, there were very few good places to eat and even fewer where you can get on the Internet. My favorite hangout became a pizza place in the small town center. Over the months that we visited Melitopol, I became a regular and the staff started trying to speak to me in English. They had the best coffee in town and access to the Net so I spent much of my free time there.

The pizza parlor's décor was somewhere between a 1950s drive-up Shoney's or Sonic and a hip little eatery in the East Village in NYC . There were plasma screens everywhere playing mostly American music videos, and the stools were covered with brightly colored naugahyde.

**My favorite pizza place (with Internet)**

The menu used pictures and unfortunately I always ended up ordering the same pizza and some kind of American coffee thing. You will never have a pizza that good anywhere on planet earth for $3. After about my 20th visit, they brought out a server from the back kitchen to take my order because he understood a bit of English. I in turn, tried to learn the Russian phrases that would support his understanding and make him look good. We always had lots of laughs when I visited them.

*January 14th*
*Melitopol, Ukraine*

Paula and I were not too worried about the court until the moment we walked into the courthouse, which was another old, dilapidated building that hadn't seen a paint job in 50 years. We knew that things could easily go awry and that the judge might turn us down for a number of reasons, including siblings, that they were two unrelated children (you cannot adopt them in Ukraine), the grandmother raising a stink, etc., etc., but it wasn't in our hands.

Have you ever been to court? I have a couple of times for various reasons, but in Ukraine, I had the feeling that the judge might walk into the room, point and accuse me of one of the bad things I did in my youth and then lock me up. It was very uncomfortable.

**The Melitopol Court**

Our appointment was at 10 a.m., so we were there 15 minutes early. At 10:30, only 30 minutes late, we were escorted into the courtroom. It was right out of a Southern Baptist church in the 1930s, or maybe like something I had seen on the Andy Griffith show. The room was adorned with thin wooden benches worn grey paint from many years of legal proceedings, floors made of hand cut boards, and naked dangling lights that hung 18 inches from the ceiling. The only thing that made it look like a courtroom was the jail cell in the middle of the room constructed of rebar, and the old Dell computer they used for recording the court proceedings.

**The Court Room waiting area... just kidding**

So we sat and sat. A representative from the orphanage and one from the inspector's office sat with us and we spoke through Vitaly. They were on hand to give testimony to the judge and their recommendation for adoption.

There were two jurors, a court reporter wearing a very low cut blouse, a female prosecutor and a sheriff. At about 11:30 a.m. the judge quickly walks into the room and starts reading, and reading, and… reading. Reading the petition word-by-word, page-by-page.

The instructions to the translator, to us, "You will address me as *Your Honor*."

He is a nicely dressed man in his late 30s, who eventually looked up briefly to acknowledge our presence.

We are then told to stand and address the court.

The judge's questions were varied, "Why do you want to adopt in Ukraine?" to "How much money do you make?"

There was nothing to worry about. Then he turned to the jurors to see if they wanted to ask us questions — which they did not and so he turned to the prosecutor who asked, "What will you do when the hard times come with the girls?"

My answers were satisfactory for all of her questions and at last the judge asked, "Would you like to say anything else?"

"Your Honor, we would like to ask the court to waive the waiting period after your decision. There are several reasons for this and we would like to get home as soon as possible." and, I continued, "My mother is almost 80 and has been taking care of our daughter for four months, my wife's father is ill and she wants to be with him, and my business is suffering having been in Ukraine for so long."

The judge listened intently and seemed to nod slightly in approval and told us he would be back in a few minutes with his decision.

An hour and a half later, we were still waiting for the judge's decision when the court secretary entered the courtroom and told us to come back after lunch.

"It's Ukraine."

We had planned to do so much including court, going to the notary, driving to Zaporizhzhya. Not anymore. We would need to be happy just to get out of court. We took our entourage to lunch at my pizza place, had an espresso returning at 2 p.m.

**Judge Michael**

Right on time (ha!) at 3 p.m., the judge walked in and again starts reading, and reading, and reading — out loud. It was like he was not breathing or something, a single monotone voice for 20 minutes reading the single-spaced multi-page document as fast as he could. Paula and I didn't understand a word except when he mentioned our names.

At one point, I turned to Paula and said, "I don't think he has mentioned Nadya." It was the only time that day when I had a negative thought, but it was a scary one.

"What if the grandmother had sent something disputing the adoption and he is going to let us adopt Albina but not Nadya?" It was crazy but it could happen. After all…

"It's Ukraine."

"It is in the court's interest to wave the mandatory 10-day waiting period due to family hardship and the extended time this couple has spent in our country already," the judge said and Vitaly translated.

Finally, when he was done reading into his tape recorder, he stood and exited the room — almost at a run.

Vitaly turned to us and simply said, **"Congratulations Michael and Paula, you have two new daughters!"**

```
BLOG Entry - It's official folks ... Paula
has given birth to two 11-year-old girls
Albina and Nadya. The Redman clan is now
five strong!


We went to court yesterday and the hearing
was very short, only 25 minutes. It was
the next seven hours of waiting that killed
us …

There is still quite a bit of work to do
like getting the birth certificates,
passports, medical papers, and the U.S.
Embassy stuff, not to mention throwing a
going away party for the girls at the
orphanage, and a bunch of other things …
but for the most part, we are wrapping up
this part of the journey.
```

```
God has been watching over us, and we thank
him for taking care of us and blessing us
with two awesome children.
Michael
```

It was over. Just like that ... in a moment

I couldn't believe we were through. Albina and Nadya were our children now.

But, all things being equal, in Ukraine you come to expect the unexpected and court was no different. The judge had disappeared to write up the decree and we expected it might take a few minutes for him to finish. What we didn't expect was that four hours later we would still be sitting there in his small courtroom waiting for him.

Occasionally Vitaly would check on his progress and they would say, "Just a few more minutes." He would return, eyes down, shaking his head. "We won't get anything done today. This is awful."

By 4:30 p.m. the courthouse was clearing out, people bundling up to face the elements and go home for the day. Just before 5 p.m., I asked Vitaly to go see the judge and find out what the problem was. He very reluctantly agreed to do so. I walked with him down the empty hallway to a waiting guard who let him through his checkpoint and allowed him upstairs to the judge's chamber. There was only one problem — the judge had gone home, too. No one told us. They just left us sitting in the courtroom for four hours.

Vitaly was told, "Come back tomorrow at 11 a.m." He was visibly upset having planned a very big paperwork day starting early the next morning but it was not to be.

After the long bittersweet day, Sasha dropped us off at the hotel where we met a wonderful American couple, Jerry and Kay, who were missionaries in Russia, spending time in Ukraine due to a recent change in the law that only allowed them to be in-country six months out of the year. They had been missionaries for 16 years and introduced us to a wonderful little Grace-based church which we attended the following Sunday.

*January 20th*
*Melitopol, Ukraine*

Paula left for Cleveland at about 6pm for the long trip home to relieve June. I stayed on with Vitaly to finish the mountains of paperwork and the processing in Kiev.

*January 23rd*
*Melitopol, Ukraine*

With Paula safely home, Vitaly and I were on our own to complete the process. We would wrap up the paperwork and then I would bring the girls home.

Up at 5:30 a.m., we drove to the orphanage to pick up the girls. I was so tired with too much to do in too-little time. When we arrived at the orphanage, we saw the girls' silhouettes moving through the shadows in the early morning darkness and into the cafeteria to find something to eat … two and a half hours of driving and we were once again at the Justice Department in Zaporizhzhya to pick up the signed birth certificates and pay them $1,000 in cash.

Next, we went to the Zaporizhzhya notary to have the birth certificates officially notarized, which took another hour and then to the passport office where we realized Dima still had the original Ukrainian passports. We paid the office manager $300 in cash to expedite the passports which he non-discreetly put in his wallet (all passports are issued in Kiev and then sent back to the local passport office which is a process that normally takes up to two weeks).

The office manager said, "You should have them next Tuesday if they get the tax number for your children." He also told us, "I need one more copy of this document from your original notary."

It seems it never ends. As usual, the girls are hungry and I was too, so we decided to stop and eat while Vitaly went to the notary to get one more copy, which of course has to be handwritten.

This time we found a little restaurant right down the street, ordered and when I finally received my food it was stuffed with mushrooms, which I like but cannot eat. After 15 more minutes, I was informed that they don't have any of what I had ordered an hour earlier.

"It's Ukraine!"

A bowl of soup will have to do.

At lunch, we also decided that the girls wouldn't attend the new church we found because some of the other children from the orphanage thought it was too long and boring. As much as I wanted to attend church with our new children, I didn't want to see the long faces they would certainly be wearing after the first 10 minutes of the service.

After the familiar long drive back to Melitopol, I went about the business of working on my tech business and spent several hours looking for potential partners for my company MyMusicSource.com.

# Orphanage Party

*January 24th*
*Melitopol, Ukraine*

Paula and I had talked many times about how we would leave Ukraine and how we might say goodbye to the children. We decided that a party for all of the kids might be the best way for us to celebrate that our girls were coming home with us and thank them. We weren't sure how to approach such an undertaking for 100 children, but thought maybe some snacks and a cake might do the trick.

Vitaly decided the best thing to do would be to meet with Valery and ask him what the children might like to eat as a treat, so we knocked on his office door and he answered with his usual big smile, in his suit and invited us in.

Vitaly explained what we had planned, "Michael would like to have a party for all of the children so they can say goodbye to Nadya and Albina."

Valery's eyes lit up as he replied, "This is a very good thing to do. The children will be so happy. You can do it at lunch time this Saturday!" as he called loudly to one of his assistants.

Marina entered the room and Valery excused himself, "I will be back in a few minutes. Please, wait here." When Valery spoke to us, we knew that we should just sit and wait.

Children walked past his office in a constant stream and poked their heads in to see what we were doing and say, "Privet!" ("Hi", in Russian) as Vitaly and I sat and wondered what Valery was discussing with Marina.

Finally, they returned to the office and handed us a list. "This is what I would like you to get for the children's party," Valery said. My mouth dropped open when I saw his list and I just had to laugh to myself. You see, Valery had never asked anything of us including an orphanage donation, which is customary in the adoption world. This was a chance for him to help the kids, and the orphanage as well.

This was Valery's list:

> 600 oranges
> 300 mandarins
> 300 apples
> 400 little cakes
> 30 gallons of assorted drinks
> 30 dozen eggs
> 100 lbs. of salami
> 300 bottles of Head & Shoulders shampoo
> Cookies, crackers, bread, and more.

"I think we can do this," I said, doing some quick math and figuring that it might be a couple of thousand dollars, but of all of the money we spent on our trips, this was the most satisfying.

"Good." Valery said. "Bring it to the back door of the cafeteria tomorrow and we will have the party the next day." And so we left.

As soon as we were outside, Vitaly asked me, "Michael, are you sure you want to do this? I think Valery is taking advantage of you."

"Of course I want to do this. It is for the kids and even if the staff is taking some home, it is still worth it to me."

"Okay, I will ask Sasha to take you tomorrow to the market and I will stay in my apartment to rewrite some paperwork," Then we drove to the hotel in relative silence.

*January 25th*
*Melitopol, Ukraine*

Sasha arrived at Seven Stars to pick me up pretty early and without Vitaly around to translate, we looked at each other a lot and smiled. I handed him the list for the party and we drove out to the internot to pick up the girls for a major day of shopping.

Now as cheap as everything is at the markets, I didn't realize that there was even another level to the underground community market that dealt in super-wholesale to the markets. I was about to get schooled in the art of buying bulk — "Ukrainian" style.

Sasha grew up in Melitopol and had been driving a taxi for 20 years so he really knew his way around. Our first stop was to a special market where the only product sold is citrus. When we pulled in, I was astonished to see well over 100 vendors bundled up, standing around fires to keep warm, with some 30 different varieties of citrus including oranges, mandarins, grapefruit, lemons, etc.

Sasha started the negotiation process by handing one of the heavily dressed men his list. He looked it over and started to tell Sasha what he has, doesn't have and what it will cost. Sasha, in turn, listens very closely and then turns and motions to me that he is not satisfied with the cost and we are going to the next vendor. We did this several times before he finally told me in sign language that he needed 1,000 greevna ($125 USD). They talked a little more about the girls and how we are adopting them and everybody shook my hand as we loaded boxes and boxes of fruit into Sasha's small car. All I could think of at this particular moment is how it's going to be impossible for us to fit everything in his 25-year-old hatchback.

Next, we found a little building hidden behind the big outdoor market that only sold cookies. We wandered around the large room that contained a small wire cage with a young man chain-smoking non-filtered cigarettes, texting and keeping one eye focused squarely on us. After a great deal of sorting through the mounds of cookie boxes, we bought about 30 dozen and loaded them into the car.

We repeated this process at a beverage shop and a vegetable market, working our way down Valery's list and feeling pretty good until we visited a few shops looking for shampoo with no luck. Finally, a woman at one of the shops gave Sasha directions to a place were we could buy shampoo and "Anything you want," pointing back into an alley amid clusters of shadowed buildings behind her.

Sasha asked that the girls stay in the car and motioned to me to follow him. We walk for a while looking at the rusted metal doors and avoiding the packs of dogs wandering the street until we came upon a building with a dark hall and no signage. I started to get nervous and uncomfortable, something just didn't feel right. I could tell that Sasha had a similar feeling but he couldn't share it verbally with me so together we walked into the darkness of the building looking for an indication that we're in the right place. This is obviously a black market operation that could be very dangerous for foreigners.

Sasha finally said, "Anne near zeds." (They are not here.) I walked out as fast as I could. Then says, "Padashdee zdees." (Wait here.)

He disappeared around a corner and I just stood where he told me and kept an eye on the dogs that were starting to circle around me. One of the biggest fears I have from childhood is being attacked by dogs so this was definitely somewhere I didn't want to be.

Fifteen long minutes later and Sasha appeared and pointed back to the same door with the long dark hallway and the racial graffiti on the walls. He motioned again to follow him and stopped at an unmarked door on the right. Without even knocking, he entered the room, which was six-feet square with three guys who are sitting on stools behind a computer … they didn't smile.

"What do you want?" one of them says in a threatening tone. Sasha started talking fast and I could feel the tension mounting as he talked ever faster.

The man behind the desk flips through a couple of large catalogs and then at the computer and said, "Give me 2,000 greevna now." I hand over the money trying not to show the wad of bills in my pocket.

"Wait outside," he said, never changing his expression and pointing to the alley.

I was perfectly happy to leave, and when we did my heart rate dropped 30 points or so. It was also a good time to go check on the girls so I weaved my way back through the maze of alleys to the car, only to find the girls asleep in the car and the door still securely locked.

Sasha, now knowing where to go, drove us closer to the building and we wait — 15 minutes, 30 minutes, one hour and then after two hours, a big rolling garage-type door started to open in the next building. A man came out and signaled to Sasha to enter. I wasn't allowed to follow but can see aisle after aisle of consumer-type products stacked 20 feet high.  It looked like a very large grocery store in a dark dimly lit warehouse.  This was a black marketer's warehouse and it became clear that they were just as leery of us as we were of them.

Sasha emerged with a small pallet of unopened boxes of shampoo.  I couldn't believe it.  They delivered exactly 300 bottles of shampoo for about 60 cents a bottle.  And, the bonus - we didn't get killed … just kidding, but there were moments when I was sure it might be a possibility.

By about 4 p.m., we headed back to the internot with the car stuffed to the gills and riding low on the highway.  When we arrived, Valery commandeered 30 children who set up a line into the commissary and gently passed each box, which was quickly deposited into a locked room.

*January 26th*
*Melitopol, Ukraine*

With the food purchased everything was in place for the going away luncheon for Albina and Nadya.  Watching every child in the orphanage line up and get ready to have a little celebration was truly moving.  You could see their excitement; they were doing something very special, something they don't experience in their day-to-day lives here at the internot.

I went inside and the chef had done a wonderful job of decorating every table and creatively placing the snacks for each child. As unbelievable as it sounds, she used all of the food we had bought the day before. This made me feel pretty good because I was sure that a high percentage of the food would end up in the teachers' homes.

The children filed into the cafeteria in one long single line and I smiled at each one as they passed. As the children were seated, they quickly started stuffing the fruit into their pockets. Food would be consumed now or maybe late tonight in the privacy of their beds.

Valery entered the room and asked if I would say a few words. I stepped forward as he quieted the kids and looked out across the room. It was an emotional moment and all I could do to open my mouth. Ninety-four kids staring directly at me with a tough story of survival of their own that they could tell. Most of the circumstances that led them to this time and place were not happy ones I can assure you, and they carried those stories on their faces and in their eyes.

Albina and Nadya stood next to me with Valery's arm around them and Marina, one of the caregivers, was by my side.

And so I started (translated by Vitaly).

"Hi kids, let's all start by saying hello to Paula into the video camera, who had to go home yesterday." All 94 children screamed, "Hi Paula!" It was deafening.

I continued, "I just want to thank you for making our visit so pleasant, each and every one of you is special." I scanned the room taking this disturbing vision of all of the children who wanted and needed families so desperately.

That's when I started losing it. My eyes flooded and I just couldn't speak for a moment. If you have ever been to an orphanage, you will know exactly what I am talking about.

Pushing through, I said, "Paula and I wanted to have a little celebration before Albina and Nadya came to America with us to be our daughters."

I lost it again, and it was getting embarrassing because these children were probably wondering what was wrong with this guy.

"We only wish our home was big enough to take all of you home with us," I continued. "We will take very good care of your friends, Albina and Nadya, and we will be back. Thank you."

It was one of the most difficult talks I have ever given. I think the only thing that kept me from stopping was looking out and seeing Nika, who had been our savior as a translator throughout our journey, in the back of the room. She was smiling and nodding her head reassuringly.

After our little celebratory meal, we headed outside to arrange for some games. The weather was miserable but we thought a race might be a good start. Conferring with Nika, we decided the best way to approach this would be age-gender-specific. The hard part was getting all of the kids to listen! Once we accomplished this, we started with the six-to-nine-year olds.

We lined them up behind a green line in the parking lot and told them they needed to run as fast as they could to the front gate of the orphanage, which was about 150 yards away and back. They were required to touch the gate and someone would be there to check that they did in fact, touch it, and then run back and touch the hand of our translator, Sveta.

So off they went; I was shocked how fast those little kids could run and they did so with so much heart. Each and every one was determined to come in first. As the first child crossed the finish line, everyone was screaming and shouting at the tops of their lungs, "Vika! Vika! Vika!"

Vika was Albina's best friend and such a nice little girl, and she could really run. I tried to act official as I shook her hand and gave her 20 greevna (about $3). She was breathing heavily, smiling broadly, and very grateful.

We continued the races [probably 10 in all] without incident until the 10 to 13-year old boys. It was a madhouse as they lined up everywhere with expressions ranging from bewilderment to sheer determination.

"Ready - Set - Wait, wait, " I said, as all the boys started to run on "Set" and had moved the green line sideways and 20 yards closer to gain an advantage over the smaller boys.

We tried a couple more times and finally "G-o-o-o-o!" They took off amazingly fast and grouped at the first corner. All of a sudden, there was a pileup and one little guy fell and was getting trampled by the other boys. We jumped to his aid as the rest of the boys, eager to win the prize money, didn't even look back.

Before we could get him up the boys were back, crossed the line and were arguing about who did, or did not, touch the gate. The little guy was crying, and I thought for sure he had broken his arm, but as it turned out, it was a mixture of pain, embarrassment, and anger at the other boys for knocking him out of the race. He was fine though and I quietly slipped him a few Greevna to ease his pain.

As expected, Nika won the final race. She was probably the best athlete and fastest runner in the orphanage.

The rain was coming down and we were debating between a chess tournament, ping-pong or both. Both ideas were ultimately panned because it was getting late and it was decided that a disco night would be just fine. Valery told the kids that there would be no studies for the rest of the day and led us into his office.

Unfortunately, about 30 minutes later, Marina entered the office and said, "The children don't have anything to do now. Should we have disco?"

Valery replied, "No, send them back to school." Of course, this was not what Marina wanted to hear because the children were spread all over the neighborhood and she, being the school's headmistress, would need to round them up.

After a couple of shots of cognac in Valery's office, we called it a day and drove back to the Seven Stars and rest.

# Goodbye Ukraine

*January 27th*
*Melitopol, Ukraine*

We called the manager at the passport agency at noon and low and behold, he had the passports in hand so we scrambled to start making arrangements for an apartment in Kiev, the flight home, and tried to book two first-class compartments on the train.

Vitaly had to take a bus and travel all the way back to Zaporizhzhya just to pick up the passports which was a six-hour trip each way and thankfully, there were no problems.  Due to the short notice, we were only able to get second-class tickets on the train, which meant that there are four beds in each compartment - so we bought all four beds.  Funny thing was that it was still cheaper than first-class … good to note for your trip.

*January 28th*
*Melitopol, Ukraine*

After an all-nighter bus trip, a weary Vitaly arrived back in Melitopol and picked me up at the hotel.  We would get the girls and start the journey to the U.S. Embassy in Kiev and onto our final destination — Cleveland, Ohio, USA!

I thanked the staff of the Seven Stars Hotel for being so kind and accommodating to us for the previous several months and climbed into Sasha's car relieved to be leaving, but strangely feeling like I might miss Melitopal. Maybe it was the food, the newness of everything we encountered, I don't know.

When we arrived at the orphanage it was still very early and there were a few children milling around but generally pretty quiet. As soon as they saw Sasha's car, they knew it was us and children started coming out of the woodwork as if some silent alarm went off. It was not long until we saw Albina running towards us with a smile from ear to ear. She snuggled right up to me and a few seconds later, was joined by Nadya.

Vitaly said, "Privet girls! We have come to take you to America." A hush fell as all of the children waited for more information, never believing this day would come. The day when some strange foreigner would come to their orphanage and take a child home with them. Today was that day, and tears flowed freely. I wasn't sure why exactly.

Were they tears of joy for the girls, tears of sadness to see them leave, or tears of longing for a family that would take them home, too?

Albina started saying her goodbyes to the multitude of friends and I took as many pictures as possible. Nadya seemed to have fewer kids to bid farewell and couldn't wait to get in the car to leave.

My friend Valery being a commanding figure — stood heads above everyone else as he approached and we started a dialog through Vitaly.

"Valery, my friend, I will never be able to repay you for the help you have given us and the friendship I feel for you," I said, sad to leave this man, with whom I had enjoyed sharing so much.

"Michael, you and Paula will take good care of my girls? I will always be your friend and I hope you can spend time with my wife and I this summer." Valery said in a very heartfelt way that seemed to come from deep inside.

With that short exchange we were ready to leave the orphanage. Vitaly and I looked for the girls and realized they had disappeared. I thought to myself that something new had crept into the picture but was relieved when I heard one of the children say, "They went to see their teacher to say goodbye."

We climbed into the car and drove into the village and to my astonishment, Vitaly directed Sasha right to the teacher's house. We knocked on the door and a woman answered and welcomed us in with tears in her eyes .

We respectfully declined her invitation to come inside because time was getting tight. I asked for the girls to come out and get in the car. It was a bit like pulling teeth, as both Albina and Nadya were very connected to this woman who had been both a mentor and a mother figure to them. After a short time, they came out of the house and everybody cried as we drove away looking for the last time at their teacher, the orphanage, the village and the children left behind. It was a bittersweet moment to say the least.

It was not long before the girls' anticipation of America was getting out of control and I was bombarded with questions about everything from, "What will our school be like?" "What kind of food does our sister Grace like?"

Vitaly and I had other things on our minds though as we planned the upcoming train trip and went through the paperwork we would need in two days for the U.S. Embassy. First on our list was a special meal on the train so we stopped at the now familiar AMC Top store.

Vitaly told me that, "In Ukraine, when people travel on the train it is customary to make a big dinner and eat on the train." So that's exactly what we did. We bought cheese, chicken cutlets, sausage (mystery meat), bread, crackers, pickles, fruit and dessert.

Once on the train, we decided that Vitaly and I would share one compartment and put the girls in the other. We packed our bags in the cramped overhead and invited the girls over to have a small feast prior to settling down for the night and I was once again amazed at the lack of leftovers.

At about 10 p.m., we sent the girls back to their compartment to go to sleep and wrapped the heating pipes under the bed so that the compartment temperature was tolerable. About midnight, we heard laughing next door and found the girls wide-awake, playing and watching TV.

"Turn out the light and go to sleep," Vitaly said and Albina agreed that they would listen to him this one last time.

# The U.S. Embassy

*January 29th*
*Kiev, Ukraine*

We arrived about 7 a.m. in Kiev, took a taxi to the apartment that Dima had arranged and then headed directly to the Embassy. I wasn't sure what to expect because I've never been to an embassy before.

The fact is, that it's not really an embassy at all, but the consulate office, which is quite different. This is the place where everybody comes to apply for a visa to come to the USA, be interviewed and they generally conduct immigration business. We arrived at 8:30 a.m. and found a small playground with a swing and slide behind the Embassy building to help pass the time while we waited for the Embassy to open. It was a cold morning, and trying to keep Nadya from getting wet and messy was a chore.

I had my camera at the ready and was quickly scolded when I attempted to take a picture of the Embassy and the American flag.

"Turn the camera off. You cannot take pictures," said the Ukrainian guard in a threatening tone. It was the first time I felt like I wanted to blow off someone in Ukraine — probably because I felt a tinge of American pride.

There were over 100 people quietly waiting in a single-file line for the consulate to open at 9 a.m. and we were hoping we wouldn't freeze to death. Dima started to hand me lots of documents while telling me what to do with them.

"Do you mean that you are not coming in with me?" I asked.

"Of course not, Michael," Dima replied.

"They do not allow me to come in." Oh, great, I thought because I hadn't been listening all that carefully.

We were also at the back of the line, which was a bummer. But then — a light at the end of the tunnel…

"Oh, you are American. You go right to the front of the line." Dima translates this … I beam … finally some justice!

There was a short security check when we walked into the consulate and then signs that directed us to adoption processing. I met a nice young Ukrainian man at the counter who was very helpful, and in about 30 minutes he sent us off, "I have everything I need from the Ukrainian government," he said. "Just bring back form 230, an extra I-600, and the medical report tomorrow morning at 9 a.m. I will have everything ready for your second interview."

We left the Embassy, grabbed a nearby cab and took off to the hospital which was only a few miles drive.

"That is the hospital where they did my heart surgery." Vitaly said pointing to a circa 1920s building with piles of garbage stacked outside obscuring the windows.

"It was expensive!" he said. "I was there for months and very, very uncomfortable. I still have problems because my heart rhythm is not steady but I can't afford the medicine now."

We pulled up to the hospital entrance, paid the driver and entered a hallway with over 200 people sitting on a long wooden bench waiting, mostly single mothers with small children and the elderly.

I said, "We will be here for hours."

Vitaly replied, "Michael, give me $20." Again, I handed over the money, used to not asking questions about the expedition fees. I already knew the drill and, as expected, Vitaly returned moments later and led us right into the doctor's office ahead of the waiting masses. I felt a bit embarrassed to move to the front of the line but it's the way business is done here and nobody even gave us a second look.

The doctor was a young man in his 30s, spoke English and was approved by the U.S. Embassy — meaning they will accept his medical opinion. He introduced himself and asked for the girls' medical records most of which are handwritten on scraps of paper, he scanned them and then started his examination. In short, he told me that the girls are in good health with no major problems.

"Nadya has been admitted to the hospital for tuberculosis but the tests seem to be negative from what I read here," he said. "But, I think we should have a chest x-ray to be sure."

The x-ray room was one of the scariest places in the hospital located deep in the basement with dark grey walls, a single dangling light bulb [which, I've come to realize is a required part of Ukrainian décor] and a general sense of despair hanging heavily in the air. The x-ray machine was at least 30 years old, and people were standing everywhere with broken bones wrapped in sheets. This place looked like a military field hospital in World War I somewhere in Southern France, or maybe the set from the TV show 'Mash'. Nadya was taken behind the thick grey metal doors and I stood in the hallway with everyone else. Strangely, there were no chairs or benches.

Thirty minutes later she came out and told me, "It was very uncomfortable and hurt when they pressed the machine on my chest." (Ukrainian for very, very scary.)

From the basement, we went to several other offices in the hospital to have blood drawn and other tests required by the Embassy. In total, the medical exam took us about three hours to complete, cost $240 U.S., and was painless, except for the drawing of blood — they still use really big needles which made both girls cry.

We were told that we needed to come back at 3 p.m. that same afternoon to pick up the chest x-ray results, so Vitaly took us back to our apartment.

At 3:30 my phone rang and a frantic Vitaly said, "Michael, this is very upsetting. They are such idiots! The administrator will not give me the papers he promised. You must come right away."

I had never heard him so upset and was worried about his heart. "What was this about?" I thought. Does Nadya have TB?

I told the girls, "I need to go back to the hospital so I would like you to stay here and watch TV. I am locking the front door and you must not open it for anyone except me," and then I went downstairs where Dima had sent a taxi to pick me up.

Twenty minutes later I arrived at the hospital to see Vitaly and Dima sitting outside the administrator's office. They were visibly upset by the current situation but they didn't even have time to explain what is going on before the door opened and I am summoned into the administrator's office.

Once in the office they closed the doors and the hospital administrator started to rant, "Who is this man, Vitaly? He is rude, demanding and I am not going to give him the x-rays. I am going to call the consulate and demand that he be reprimanded. We have never been treated like this."

On and on he went for five minutes without taking a breath. It was obvious that Vitaly had reached his boiling point — as many of us do when you have just had enough. Vitaly had had enough of the old Soviet, which was, do not ask questions and do as you were told. Waiting and hoping to get action in Ukraine is a way of life here.

I spent the next 20 minutes apologizing to the administrator and assuring him I would talk to Vitaly, he would apologize, and it would never happen again. He finally handed me the x-rays and told me the results were negative.

"Nadya does not have tuberculosis." This was a tremendous relief. "You may go now, but tell Vitaly he may never, ever come back to our hospital." I smiled and walked out of the office.

Dima and Vitaly were still sitting in the hall with grave looks of concern on their faces. They thought I had been called because the results of the x-ray were positive and Nadya was very sick, but they quickly smiled when I told them,

"They were just mad at us. Nadya is okay."

It had been a long day and we were exhausted and so when I arrived back at the apartment, I just grabbed the girls and we walked down the street to have a simple dinner of borscht and potatoes.

Before we went to bed, I sat with the girls in their oversized nightgown tee shirts and looked out the window in my room at a wonderful fireworks display that was taking place over at the new national soccer stadium that was under construction just across the street. It went on for 30 minutes and I couldn't even look at it. All I could do was stare at the girls and reflect on how far we had come in the past five months.

Coming to Ukraine had been a real emotional roller coaster that, on many occasions, Paula and I thought would end in disaster. At some point, God stepped in, took over and had given us the strength to continue even when we wanted to give up. The end result was the adoption of Nadya and Albina, which even in our wildest dreams we couldn't have imagined would happen. I was so thankful. The fireworks were a celebration of our new daughters, our new family — God had directed this great gift.

*January 30th*
*Kiev, Ukraine*

I woke up early and walked what seemed like two miles to get a cup of the "now world-famous McDonald's coffee" … famous, at least, in my mind.

Dima and Vitaly picked us up for the last time to go to the Embassy, and within an hour we had the girls' visas and were done, and I do mean *done*.

We were going home now.

Home to the USA.

After lunch, I said goodbye to Vitaly, the man who had become more than our facilitator; he was our friend. A friend who had always put our needs before his own. He was on his way to the train station to head home to Nikolayev and his own family. He had become part of our family along the way and I will miss him.

# Home at Last

*January 31st*
*Kiev, Ukraine*

"Goodbye, Kiev," I said with a smile as we opened the taxi door.

"Goodbye, Dima. Thank you for all that you have done for us. Without your help, our girls would still be sitting in the orphanage in Melitopol wondering what happened to the American couple that said they would come back and take them home."

"Have a safe trip home," said Dima. And we left for the airport.

Once in the airport, it was a right turn to the International Flights entrance, and the start of an hour and a half of border control where they read every line of the court decree and closely scrutinize the exit visas before eventually letting us pass to the holding area and the departure gates.

We were now in familiar territory sitting at the gate, the same gate we have visited on every trip here. The girls were excited and spent the next two hours calling everybody they knew to say goodbye including our taxi driver, Sasha.

Our final flight home was blessedly without drama — watching movies and trying to stay comfortable on the 11-hour flight.

At 11:37 a.m., we arrived at the Cleveland Hopkins Airport. Paula and Grace were patiently waiting for us in baggage claim and a new future was beginning to unfold.

# One Year Later

*March, 2010*
*Chagrin Falls, Ohio*

Our experience in Ukraine was not unique. As I have talked to, and connected with, other adoptive parents who have shared their stories with me, there is always some thread of their experience that was very similar to ours.  The Ukrainian children are wonderful, the justice system still in development, the State Department of Adoption [SDA] is uninformed and the process confusing and ever-changing.

It is my sincere hope that in some small way I have helped you understand the delicate nature of the Ukrainian adoption process especially if you might be a future adoptive parent of one or more of these children.  I must say that I miss Ukraine, the people and the food.

In the year since I started writing this book, we have experienced many wonderful revelations, as well as the trials of foreign adoption and in many ways, have come full circle.

First, the language lessons and the Rosetta stone program proved to be a blessing and a curse. The blessings include the progress the girls made in short order and their excitement as they both learned and practiced new English words. The challenging side has been the entire process of having an ongoing, scheduled English language program.

Paula and I understood just how hard it would be for the girls to enter the public school system and even with the ESL [English as a second language] program they were at first, overwhelmed. We had a routine that included 30 minutes a day each, with the Rosetta English program and then two to three privately tutored English sessions per week. This was in addition to the hour a day at school with the ESL program.

The pressure quickly became too much and, at times, we experienced pushback from the girls. But, we pressed on and within 3 months they had made incredible strides learning English.

One of the more enjoyable sides of adding two new family members was getting to share experiences and adventures with Albina and Nadya and watch them soak it all in.

We vacationed in Florida and New Mexico, dined at restaurants where they tried new foods including Sushi, Indian, and Mexican cuisine, some with mixed results. We ice-skated, roller-skated, bowled, fished, canoed, hiked, snow skied, and on and on. Reliving many things that we take for granted here in America was amazing.

Then Paula and I started to notice a new dynamic that slowly crept into our household. Anger, and infighting between the girls was becoming a daily routine. Things were starting to get uncomfortable and Nadya in particular seemed very unhappy.

After much discussion we decided to have her evaluated by a Russian-speaking psychiatrist who, by the way, can be almost impossible to find.

On our first visit we were told that Nadya was not the problem and she was fine. It was Paula and I and our inability to handle three children. We were very frustrated as you might expect and questioned ourselves in every way. That was on a Friday, and on Sunday evening when we returned home from the days outing there was a message on the phone. It was the psychiatrist who said, "Michael and Paula, I am very sorry to bother you on the weekend but you must come to my office Monday morning. I have made a terrible mistake and it is very important that I talk to you."

Monday morning we met and she explained that after looking at the test results much closer she would now diagnose Nadya with post-traumatic stress disorder, anxiety disorder, and something else with depression. How could she have missed this we thought, and although we were somewhat relieved that we were not seeing things, it was shocking to say the least.

Nadya was put on medication and we were referred to several psychologists. After many meetings we were presented with a plan of two to three weekly sessions that may last for five years and with no guarantee that Nadya would get better. You see, these were conditions relating to the many traumatic events in Nadya's life from ages two to seven that were deeply honed as survival skills.

Without going into great detail, we made a very hard family decision to find her a new family. It would be impossible to give all three girls the attention they needed if all of our time was devoted to one child. Grace and Albina would suffer and we wouldn't be doing Nadya any favors either.

Trying to explain this decision to others, especially our own family, was devastating because they only saw Nadya, the happy child. They believed, like the psychiatrist, that Paula and I were just in over our heads. Eventually everything calmed down but it took its toll on us.

Nadya now lives in New Jersey with a wonderful couple, an older Russian sister and is doing very well.

Another thing that has come from our experiences in Ukraine is a deep desire to help the other children at our orphanage in Melitopal.

Not long after we returned home I contacted the director, Valery and asked for pictures of all of the children we met. With the help of Frontier Horizons fifteen the other Melitopal children were hosted over the 2009 summer vacation and several have been adopted. The floodgates have opened and now many of our kids in Melitopal have families and a future.

Probably the most exciting event since leaving Ukraine is happening right now. Remember earlier in the book we met Julia

M? Her new name is Lia. She was our second adoption attempt in Melitopal. Well, as I write this we are in Denver visiting her with her new parents Victoria and Martin. We have now come full circle and experienced first hand, Gods grace.

**Julia M and Julia R**

# Grace's thoughts about our adoption

I thought you might be interested in what our daughter, Grace, was thinking about our adoption.

In her words:

"My name is Grace Redman and I am 9 years old.

When my parents said they were going to adopt again I thought they were crazy. Perhaps it was a trick to make me NOT stick my head in a book (which indeed occupies 99% of my time). But, after thinking about it I thought it was a good idea. So I asked if it would really truly happen and this time was not just about my reading all the time.

Although they would appreciate it if I didn't read quite so much. I told them that would not happen.

I have my reasons…

Let's admit it. As much as I love my parents, it is true that they are aging and most (not my grandma June, she's the coolest person in the family) old people are no fun after 50. I don't have anybody to play with so I am usually lonely. And finally, I don't have a lot of friends so a sister would be awesome.

When my parents said, "We are going to be hosting" I thought, good I'll get to meet my sisters. But as soon as they arrived I began to feel jealous and mad, sad and confused as I watched my parents dote over some girls I had never seen in my life.

I began to question my parents and ask, "Do you really love me?" But the upside was I had 2 new friends, who would gladly play with me, so my days became more filled with light and less lonely.

Finally I began to love my sisters more and more and happy that they were here. I admit, we did still fight, but I was glad I had 2 new sisters that loved me, and six months later I loved them more than anything."

~ Grace

# Albina's Story

In her own [English] words.

"I was born in Zaporizhzhya and we lived in a dormitory in one room. There were four of us, my brother, me and my mom and dad. We had a TV and 2 beds, but there was not kitchen or bathroom.

There was only one kitchen for everybody and two bathrooms. The poor people stayed on one side of the dormitory and people that had some money lived on the other side in bigger rooms. The people with some money was able to make their bathroom look nicer.

[Michael] Where did your food come from?

Well everybody cooked their own food but sometimes we didn't have anything to cook or to eat all day because my mom and dad drinking too much vodka, and my brother and me did not eat.

I had a couple of friends in the dormitory and sometimes we were playing but not too much because there was other people were sleeping.

I didn't go to school or anything but my dad was smarter than my mom and he got me a notebook and tried to home school me. I was about six and they didn't have enough money for me to go to school so he showed me how to write and letters.

My dad does not have a job because his back is broken. He actually have to be in a wheelchair. He tries to make money but men who is like in wheelchair or has problems they pay you each month very little money. But he was working a little. When my mom and dad go to the garden and they ask you to pick cherries or apples and you have to pick as many as you can and they will give you money.

It's hard because sometimes my dad goes by himself because mom, she drinks too much. I remember one time dad was really upset and he hide money from her because she always spending money on vodka and she destroy all our furniture, but we did not have much furniture. She was looking in his boots and coat pockets, and pants but I knew where it was because dad hide and I see. She hit me for not telling her where it was.

My parents where always fighting and saying bad words and once dad broke mom's nose and I had to clean up the blood. Then he did not have a wheelchair. I am screaming and they are hitting each other and I say stop and then they hit me and my mom has a black eye. When moms nose is broken it is bleeding so hard and I have to get a newspaper because we don't have any tissue or anything to wipe the floor.

My little brother is screaming when they fight and the neighbors come and take him from my parents.

I lived in this dormitory my whole life in one room and when my big sister Veronica comes there is five of us and we have to sleep on the floor.

When I was six the neighbors told the police about my mom and dad and how they fighting all the time. The police said they are going to keep and eye on them and he said " If it happens again the children will go to the " I don't know where.

So another time time my mom was drinking too much and was sleeping on the floor and I had to clean the kitchen. I was embarrassed to have other people see our room so I took the bowls to the kitchen and cleaned then and brought back. You know and then some woman or man came a write something on a piece of paper and left.

The next day my mom was ok and not drunk. We had a nice day and some tea with some sweet bread. It was nice and somebody called and the little bell rang. Dad says nobodies here. I said I will go look and there were two people not like police but a man and a woman. OK here is the paper. We are going to take your kids away to the hospital. Well my mom got upset because today she was not drunk and cared about us a little.

How come you are taking them because they are not sick or anything, and they said yes they are and he showed to my father government papers to prove he could take us. He showed them very fast and took away so my dad could not read them. He said I didn't see anything and the people said it will just be for one week and OK. Mom just packed me. I remember - it was February 17, 1990.

I remember this date because the next day was my birthday.

Before that they took us away and said not which hospital we going to. The next day my mom came and she was not drunk thank goodness. She brought me some new clothes like clean ones so I can wear them.

She brought a little thing and kasha, and very good soup and apples for my birthday. She came to see me everyday for a week. They not allowed to come in so they talk to me through the window. I feed my brother and he throws up the food and the nurse says to throw all the food away because he got sick she think it is bad food.

And then my parents came every day and some nice people gave me a Barbie and a little piano for my brother. My brother took the Barbie and tried to chew her hair off. Then when my dad saw us he said do not talk to those people - who are they, they will think we do not take care of you. He yelled at me a lot and then the last day my mom asked what can she bring for me and I said I want apples and gum. It was my first gum and I liked it.

Then some people came in and told me to pack my bags "You are going to the orphanage"

Then I got really, really upset and turned my bed upside down - I did not want to leave my brother because I loved him and took care of him. I tried to teach him how to walk because he could not walk yet. Mom didn't care about him or maybe she did but she always drunk so I had to take care of him. I was crying.

I went to an orphanage, but not really an orphanage, it was kind of a place before you go to the real orphanage."

When I find out about the new orphanage, and go there I was scared of the director because he looked scary. He was very nice though and tough but in a nice way. When he tells you to do something you do it, and when you do something wrong you in big troubles. If you drink alcohol you go to this special hospital for crazy people. Their food is very bad, awful and then they come back. If you do it again you go back.

When you get sick there is a nurse lady and she takes care to the children and if you sick or have a fever you go to a special room. If you get worse they go to the hospital. I went to hospital with a terrible cough and throwed up. I was there for four days. I didn't really want to stay there.

A day at the orphanage is like this.

First you get up at 7 and get dressed, make your bed, and then go outside and then stand in line holding hands like soldiers. Then the teacher comes and takes us to have breakfast. For breakfast we have bread, tea maybe and cheese or salami. Breakfast and dinner are the best. Sometimes oatmeal but I don't like it. The best breakfast ever is salty fish, potatoes, and beets, and butter. It's the best, but we don't have it too much. We have eggs sometimes too. and milk with noodles.

Then we go back and do our chores and make sure everything is straight. Marina always come check on us to see if we do a good job. If your room is clean you get points. If you finish your room fast you get to watch TV until it's time to go to school.

Schools starts at 8:30 am. First we have reading and then recess for 5 minutes and then math and recess for 10 minutes. Next art and recess for 15 minutes, and we have recess after every subject.

Older kids set the tables for lunch. Then we have our lunch and go back to our room. When we were small in first grade we went to the bed for a couple hours. I don't like that. Its better now.

After later at 4 o'clock we go back to school and do our homework. Then dinnertime at 6 or 7 and then we watch TV.

Every Saturday we had Disco with a disk and do DJ until 9.

The people come on Saturday and talk about God and stories. They just regular people that volunteer to come help us.

Valerie's daughters, daughter always play with me and one time the older kids that are getting out of the orphanage because it is their last year they have a party for them. There is so much food and things to drink but not alcohol just like lemonade. It's really fun. And then they have a disco. The teachers and the director dance with just them, nobody else. The little kids cannot come, but I was with his grand daughter and so I was dancing with her. It was the best day ever. She went to see the director and told me to wait for her. One of the teachers came over and yelled at me " What are you doing here, get out, get out" I said I was with her daughter but I have to go to bed. It was still the best day.

When the kids leave they go to college, but sometimes they don't go anywhere and have troubles.

There are problems sometimes in the orphanage. When I was in the orphanage I smoked in the third grade because everybody smoked. I did not want to but my friends said, "Ah, come on" I so I did and I got sick and throw up. I quit because somebody told me that you are going to adopt me. A lady in the office told me. I said "Really."

There was a bad boy that when he was angry he beat up kids, and there was one bad teacher and she had a husband and he had this mother and she was so evil. You know Nadya, well she kinda bossing another girl Julia and somebody told on her. So, she grabbed her and shook her and said "Don't you dare to say anything to her" She was really mean. She wasn't even a teacher she just lived in the apartments Also American people, they send toys and gifts to us and this teacher she comes and does not give them to us. She wants to trade them to us for money.

I would like to tell something to people that might want to adopt kids here in Ukraine. If anyone wants to adopt from Ukraine and the teachers say they are very bad children. Maybe it's true but when you in orphanage you don't have great life and kids being mean to you, and you scared. Kids will get changed when you love them so it will be ok for you."

~ Julia (Albina)

---

Julia (Albina) couldn't have said it any better. Our adoption was not the smoothest, or the shortest, but our lives have changed in many positive ways. Julia's, Nadya's and Lia's lives have been changed forever.

We believe there is no better way to serve our lord than to take care of his children and are eternally grateful for the opportunity.

Please join our Face Book Group:

## Ukraine Adoption

# Best Advice and Lessons Learned

We spent over three months in Ukraine in 2009 and the following may be helpful if you are planning a trip there.

## FOOD AND RESTAURANTS

Traveling to any foreign country can be quite upsetting to your normal routine and especially to your diet. My wife, Paula, has some recurring digestive issues and being a nutritional counselor, we were looking for good healthy food. What we found was both scary and wonderful.

Generally, the Ukrainian people eat lots of meat, potatoes, cheese, and vegetables. It became obvious to us that since we didn't speak Russian and they use the Cyrillic alphabet, we were in big trouble. The great news is that due to Ukraine's rich agriculture, the soil is full of minerals, and the produce is far superior to anything you will find in the States. The food is truly organic because farmers cannot afford the pesticides, fertilizers and other chemicals that we tend to use here so freely.

You will find their coffee to be similar to European espressos, and the best place I found to buy coffee was, believe it or not, McDonald's. It is fresh-ground and costs about 80 cents. You will only find McDonald's in the large cities like Kiev. There are no Starbucks in Ukraine. Most people drink instant coffee, which if you get the Nestles brand, you will find that it's not too bad.

Let's talk restaurants -

If you are not with a translator, ask the host if they have an English menu. Many do, until you get into some of the smaller towns and villages.

What we did was sit with Vitaly on one of our first days and had him read everything on the menu. Paula made notes of everything we could eat and then Vitaly wrote it in Russian phonetically. It was helpful and got us through many meals.

You will find most of the bigger towns have lots of pizza places, etc., but I encourage you to eat in local restaurants. The soups are great, including borscht, which I thought was just beet soup — I don't like beets — but includes many other ingredients. Many of the salads are made with mayo but can be very tasty (<u>Ochin</u> <u>Facusna</u> in Russian).

**Try ordering things like:**

*Meat Soup* (Soylanka)

*Borscht* — It's not just beet soup and it is very tasty.

*Chicken Cutlet* — I liked this chicken. It's a lightly battered, butterflied chicken breast.

*Vegetable salads* — They may call this Mediterranean, Vegetable, or Greek salad. These are wonderful salads with red pepper, olives, pine nuts, lettuce, cheese, etc.

*Potatoes* — fried, boiled with cheese (and not usually greasy).

*Omelets* — They do not serve breakfast in most of Ukraine but I often ordered a great little crêpe-type of omelet with spinach and cheese.

*Fish* — We did not eat much fish, but Ukraine is renowned for their herring and smoked fish.

*Water* — Ukrainians like mineral water that is carbonated. You can try it but we didn't like it because the slightly salty taste and warm bubbles do nothing for me. Paula and I drank exclusively Bon Aqua purified water. It is a Pepsi [we don't drink soda] product and clean. It can be found in most any kiosk or grocery. Get the one with the light-blue top, which indicates that it is not carbonated.

## GROCERY STORES

All of the bigger cities and towns have multiple markets, but just about any store can be called a market. Most stores have good cheese, yogurt, bread, crackers and general supplies. You should definitely try the fruit juices, as you will not find a juice in the U.S. that tastes as good — guaranteed.

## LOCAL MARKETS

It took us about two weeks to discover the local outdoor markets. Every town has one or more. You will find everything you can imagine from milk right from the cow to produce, fish, meat, hardware, clothes, junk, snacks, and even an underground money exchange if you ask your taxi driver.

There are individual kiosks that are open seven days a week. In Melitopol, which is a small town, there were two outdoor markets. The larger market had probably 500 booths and could take you a half-day just to walk it. We shopped at these markets most everyday. It is truly a treasure that you won't experience at home. We took the girls there to buy clothes and we would buy large bags of desserts to take to the orphanage for 75 kids for $6 — you must go. Try to get your apartment or hotel within easy walking distance of the market.

## ADOPTION AGENGIES

1. It is not a requirement to hire an agency to adopt in Ukraine. You can hook up with a good hosting company that is typically in the business of helping children. Making a living is their secondary mission. We were lucky enough to work with Frontier Horizon and they helped us navigate the Ukrainian system. They don't have facilitators on staff but do have connections — in our case, it was Dima.

Working with a hosting company has many advantages in that you host your potential new daughter or son and get to see how the family chemistry works prior to committing to adoption.

You can also walk into the SDA appointment with a petition for a specific child, which can make things easier.

Another advantage is cost. The cost of working with a hosting company will be about 60% less than using an agency [who outsource everything anyway].

Now, this direct hosting route is not for everybody. There are many, many reputable adoption agencies that put the child's welfare at the top of the list and bend over backwards to help you and your family. Your decision should be based upon your own personal needs.

I would say that you should check out every company Agency or Hosting thoroughly before making a decision. A good place to start is on blogs and forums.

**THE SDA MEETING**

You really don't need to pack your "go to meeting" clothes or get dressed up as we were told. My wife and I brought special outfits to wear for this meeting only to be met by our facilitator who was wearing jeans and a tee shirt. The meeting with the SDA is really just one or maybe two psychologists asking a few quick questions and then they show you pictures from which to choose your child.

Be prepared to answer the basic questions:
- Why do you want to adopt in Ukraine?
- What do you do for a living?
- How much money do you make?
- Do you have other children?
- What will you do when you get home and the child is a problem?

## **PAPERWORK**

*Notary* - A notary in Ukraine is much different than you might be used to. They are lawyers that are responsible for creating legal documents and filing them, not just a person that validates your signature. Many of the documents you need in the process will require notarization. The trick in all of the small towns will be finding a notary with experience in adoptions. Once you have found a notary, they will handwrite or type many of the documents you will need.

*Inspectors* - Each town has a bunch of officials including inspectors that are responsible for the orphanages and allowed to interpret many of the laws locally. When you receive your referral, you will travel to a town and the first thing you must do is go to the local inspector's office (usually a female) and present your referral. In some cases, they will ask you questions, much like the SDA, and then arrange for you to see the child. Most of the time they will tell you that they need to be present at every meeting but this is only to see if you are to be trusted. Usually after the first day or so, they waive this requirement.

If splitting up siblings is involved, as was our case, you will need the inspector's permission to do this. It is done at their discretion.

## YOUR CHILD

Don't just stand idly by and take for granted that you are receiving accurate information regarding the child's health, siblings or anything else. Ask lots of questions [write them down] and push to get the answers. Most of the people we came in contact with were telling us what they believed to be true; however, often their information was just dead wrong.

3. You also need to understand that adoption is very big business for everyone involved so finding a child and pushing the transaction through the system quickly is how facilitators make their living. Make sure that what is written in the child's profile is correct and make your acceptance of the child contingent upon this information with the SDA upfront. If possible try to speak to the orphanage director personally, and also to the child prior to any long-distance travel.

The kinds of questions might be:

- How long has the child been at your orphanage?
- Do you know the parents?
- Do they have any siblings that you know of?
- Does anyone come to visit?

## INVESTIGATE!

Dig as deep as you can to find out about your child's siblings before you travel. On many occasions, we met adoptive couples whose hearts were broken because of a sibling relationship that was unknown, or that the siblings were unwilling to allow their sister/brother to be adopted.

## THE COURT DATE

You typically must pay for your court date. The judge has a lot of latitude when it comes to setting your court date. [I believe he can set your court date for up to three months from the date of submission.] Judges know you would like to get home as soon as possible. It will usually cost you between $1,000 and $2,500 depending on several factors including how the judge is feeling that day.

In some cases, the judge will quietly waive the 10-day waiting period for an extra donation. I understand that this practice has now been suspended due to an angry grandmother who got in the way of the adoption process for an Italian family, that wanted to adopt a wonderful little girl we knew named Sasha.

The waiting period is the time given to allow other family members or whoever might oppose the adoption to raise their objections or concerns with the court. In our case, Nadya's grandmother could have been a big problem by coming to court to protest her adoption. Even with her alcohol issues, the judge always rules in favor of the relatives. That's why we went to talk to her to obtain her permission, even though she had no legal rights.

You may or may not have to bring your child to the court — this depends on the region and the judge. We have been told on good authority that children as young as five have been asked to attend the hearing, where the judge will ask them if they want to be adopted, as well as other questions, so be prepared.

## EXPEDITION FEES

The Ukraine adoption system is largely based on "payola." You must pay in this country to get anything done. Government officials look the other way because they would rather the Americans, or whoever, pay the judges, inspectors, etc., than have to raise their salaries. This is widely accepted. Your facilitator will probably budget about $2,000 U.S. in cash to the local facilitator to pay fees. This might include $150 to an inspector, candy and liquors to a secretary, and in some cases, $1,000 or more to the judge who will tell your facilitator how much they desire to set a speedy court date. Don't be surprised by any of this, as it is the way the system works and how business is done. Unfortunately, some people take the money and then do not do what they say they will do.

Early on, when we were having trouble, a well-connected friend of ours in Moscow offered to help by having his friend, who was in a top position of the Kiev city council intervene on our behalf.

We were excited until we heard that he had talked to the head of the SDA and now believed that the entire Ukraine adoption system was created to bilk foreigners out of money. Now we know that this is not entirely true, but it didn't feel too good hearing it from a Ukrainian official.

You will also be expected to pay $1,000 — give or take — to the orphanage as a gift at the end of your adoption. If you are like us you will want to do much more. We really don't consider this the part of the payola system.

**What you must know about referrals and other things that our first facilitator failed to mention.**

After our second failed referral, we were encouraged by our facilitator to petition for a third referral, and if that did not work, to appeal.  Here are the facts as presented to us in a two-minute meeting we had with the deputy director of the SDA after we were told (by inside sources) that our petition had been turned down.

"A couple will ONLY receive two referrals maximum — end of story.  It is the law."

As soon as the paperwork is stamped, it counts.  It does not matter if you received bad information from the SDA, the orphanage director lied, the child tells you that they do not want to be adopted by anybody, or teachers are saying bad things about you that aren't true.

None of that matters.

All of these issues came up and the SDA deputy director simply said, "I am sorry. It is the law. There is nothing I can do for you. We have never given a third referral. If you are adopting in Ukraine, you should have known the law. You are done here. Go home."

Hmm... wonder why our facilitator didn't tell us any of this going in, and wonder why he didn't even attend our second referral meeting considering it was such an important one. The list of what we were not told is very long. I tried to cover as many of those little issues as I could throughout this book.

*\*\*A referral is only a paper transaction. There is no guarantee that the child will be anything like you are told [another reason to use a hosting company vs. an agency.] Also, the notes that are included on the child's paperwork that tell you about their personality have no relevance as they are written by various people and are many times second, or third-hand information.*

## DON'T TALK TO THE CHILDREN

Another little-known fact is that you are not allowed, by law, to contact or even talk to any child other than the one you are referred to. Try to spend 10 days in an orphanage with children meeting your car, following you everywhere you go, including the restroom, and NOT get close to every child. How ridiculous is that!

Paula and I met two beautiful children in the Melitopol orphanage that wanted desperately to go home with us and join our family. We fell for them as well. Konstantin vigorously encouraged us to spend as much time as we could at the orphanage with these girls, not once telling us that we could never ask for their referrals because we met them illegally, and that the orphanage director could even be prosecuted for having allowed it.

## MEDICAL TREATMENT

Some simple advice about medical treatment… If you are sick or injured in Ukraine, catch the first plane home. I'm not kidding. The medical system is corrupt and is a total mess as far as we are concerned. This not meant to be a slam to the government — it's just the way it is. If you don't have a lot of money, they might let you die, as was the case with a close friend's daughter.

His daughter's story is tragic. She was only six when they diagnosed cancer. One hour before she was to have surgery the anesthesiologist walked into the room and demanded $5,000 U.S., saying, "You daughter may not receive enough anesthesia otherwise."

My friend did not have the money and negotiated a lesser amount that proved to not be enough. When his daughter awoke in intensive care, she started having problems breathing and her father screamed, "Help, help, my daughter is not breathing," but nobody came. The doctor had gone home and there were no nurses. His daughter died in his arms. This is a tough country.

## HELPFUL TIDBITS

### Apartments versus Hotels

Apartments are generally your best bet depending on where you are going, as many of the smaller towns just don't have hotels. Apartments can be rented by the day, and come in all varieties from one room to multiple bedrooms. It is important to find a good broker to help you because you might end up in a real dump, paying a fortune. We have now stayed in at least eight different apartments in different cities most of which have been very nice. But beware of the "Internet promise" as I call it. This is when you rent an apartment that says it includes Internet [broadband] and one of any number of issues get in the way of your actually using it.

This first happened to us in Donetsk, where very few rental apartments have any Internet access. Vitaly found a broker who was a fast talker and he took us to a one-bedroom apartment. When we arrived, it had no beds at all, just a foldout sofa, and no Internet. He told us it was going to be installed in the next day or so, but that I needed to pay for it upfront. I reluctantly agreed to the $125 installation fee, but the more we talked, the further away the install date moved, until the following day when we were told that it could be 10 or more days, and there was no real guarantee. "It's Ukraine," he said.

Two other times we arrived at an apartment in Kiev only to find that the Internet didn't work. My suggestion is to ask when you rent an apartment if the fee will be reduced if the Internet does not work.

When we were in Melitopol, the apartments were awful and Vitaly was able to find us two hotels. Both were very nice, with a great little staff that tried to take care of us despite the language barrier. The first hotel did not have Internet and after five days of walking 20 minutes to a pizza place to get an Internet connection, we moved to a wonderful little hotel called Seven Stars in the city center. It cost a bit more but had wireless Internet [it didn't work in our room but worked well in the tiny lobby.]

**Street Crossings**

There are two types of street crossings in Ukraine — one with a traffic signal which you must wait for and the second which is multiple horizontal white lines crossing the street with no signal.

When you see the crossing with the multiple lines traffic must stop (and they do) for every pedestrian.

**Tipping**

We have been told many stories and eaten in every kind of restaurant in Ukraine. I have watched the locals, and typically, they do not tip. Nevertheless, I tipped between five and 10 percent. The food is very cheap and most people take extra time to try to help you figure out the menus so they really deserve it.

**Language**

It is rare to find anybody outside the major cities that speaks any English at all. You will not enjoy your trip if you do not know at least a few words in Russian. Once a local determines you're trying to speak their language, they will do everything they can to help you – including using their hands – to understand.

**Trains**

Travel to many cities outside Kiev will require that you go by train or bus. Forget the bus for long trips, as they just aren't comfortable. Buses are cheap and work for a trip of three hours or less but beyond that, my vote is to skip them.

Trains, on the other hand, are not too bad … not good, but not too bad. They are inexpensive and always on time. The trick with trains is to travel first-class. A first-class compartment has what amounts to two very small beds and a fold-down table. It is not expensive by American standards and private.

Avoid eating the treats that are in your compartment as it works like a mini bar in a hotel — convenient but very expensive. The conductor places the snacks in the compartments to earn additional money. Your best bet is to bring food with you and hand the treats back to the conductor as you settle in.

If first-class is not available or you are traveling with more than two people, you can buy second-class tickets, which are almost the same as first-class, except there are four bunks. Remember that if there are three of you, you'll still be paying for four beds but it is very affordable.

On our trip home with the girls, we bought two second-class compartments [totaling eight beds] and the price was about the same as one first-class.

## Taxis

Taking a taxi is easy in Ukraine. Just remember to either negotiate the fee upfront or make sure the driver has a meter. Otherwise, you will have to pay him anything he wants because you can't speak enough Russian to argue the point!

We made friends with Sasha, our driver in Melitopol. He drove an old wreck with windows that didn't roll down, and every so often, he would just pull over to the side of the road, get out and lift the hood. After banging for a minute or two he would get back in the car and away we would go.

Sasha always used a meter and we had him drive us all day for $30 to $40 U.S. Sasha took us everywhere we needed to go and that was a pretty good price.

After he had driven us for two weeks, he picked us up one morning and showed us that he had fixed his windows, and more repairs were on the way.

At the end of every day, I would pay him and give him a small tip. He was always embarrassed to take the tip and on one occasion when he took us to the train station, he waited an hour with us, put us on the train, and then would not accept any payment at all.

# NOTES

# NOTES

www.ingramcontent.com/pod-product-compliance
Lightning Source LLC
Chambersburg PA
CBHW061635040426
42446CB00010B/1426